IN THE FULLNESS OF TIME

Stephen Douglas Wilson

BROADMAN PRESS
NASHVILLE, TENNESSEE

© Copyright 1991 • Broadman Press
All Rights Reserved
4260-31
ISBN: 0-8054-6031-4
Dewey Decimal Classification: 225.91
Subject Headings: BIBLE. N.T.—SOCIAL LIFE AND
CUSTOMS // JESUS CHRIST
Library of Congress Catalog Number: 90-39208
Printed in the United States of America

Library of Congress Cataloging-in-Publication Data

Wilson, Stephen Douglas, 1952-
    In the fullness of time / Stephen Douglas Wilson.
    p.   cm.
    Includes bibliographical references.
    ISBN 0-8054-6031-4
    1. Jesus Christ—Biography—Early life. 2. Bible. N.T. Gospels-
-History of contemporary events. 3. Jews—History—156 B.C.-135
A.D. I. Title.
BT310.W55 1991
232.92—dc20   90-39208
                                          CIP

To my mother and father
who first exposed me to the subject of this book

Contents

List of Figures   vi

Acknowledgments   vii

Introduction   ix

1. The Time Approaches   11

2. In the Days of Caesar Augustus   25

3. The Birth of Jesus   37

4. Circumcision of Jesus and Presentation in the Temple   52

5. The Visit of the Magi   60

6. Sojourn in Egypt   76

7. The Childhood of Jesus   87

8. The "Silent Years": Thirteen to Thirty   97

Conclusion   115

Appendix 1   119

Appendix 2   120

Notes   121

List of Figures

Figure 1
Eight Annunciations of the Birth of Christ . . . 14

Figure 2
The Julio-Claudian Emperors of Rome . . . 26

Figure 3
Six Herodian Rulers of Palestine (40 B.C.-A.D. 70) . . . 28

Figure 4
Censuses of Augustus . . . 32

Figure 5
Proposed Chronology of Events Surrounding
the Birth of Christ . . . 47

Figure 6
The Early Travels of Jesus and His Family
During His Infancy . . . 54

Figure 7
Known Biblical Family Members and
Relatives of Jesus . . . 101

Acknowledgments

I wish to thank a number of people who helped me during the writing of this book. First of all, I would like to acknowledge the help of my readers and typists in both Lexington and in Pippa Passes, Kentucky. These include my two church pastors, Ross Range and Mike Caudill; my friend, Hershael York; my manuscript stylist Charlene Bentley, and my two Lexington typists, Eva Covington and Pam Thomas.

Secondly, I want to recognize the special help of my academic assistant Mitzi Crisp. Mitzi virtually took over the day-to-day management of my manuscript by providing me with research materials, reading and retyping the work, and assisting with the process of organizing the material. Her involvement made my work much easier, and I am grateful.

Finally special thanks are due to my wife Karen Ann Wilson. Pursuing both a career as well as raising our two children, Karen found the time to be a valuable part of this work. Her encouragement and prayers strengthened me during the years of preparing this book. She emerged as one of my best readers and stylists and also typed an earlier version of the manuscript. She closely shared the joys and frustrations of this project and had great faith in my ability to finish this undertaking. Thank you for tolerating such a preoccupied husband.

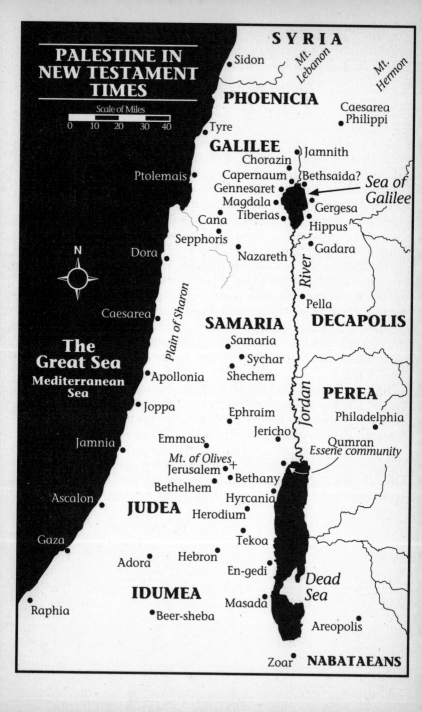

PALESTINE IN NEW TESTAMENT TIMES

Scale of Miles
0   10   20   30   40

SYRIA

Sidon

Mt. Lebanon

Mt. Hermon

PHOENICIA

Caesarea Philippi

Tyre

GALILEE

Jamnith

Chorazin

Ptolemais

Capernaum

Bethsaida?

Sea of Galilee

Gennesaret

Magdala

Gergesa

Cana

Tiberias

Hippus

Sepphoris

Gadara

Nazareth

Dora

Jordan River

Pella

SAMARIA

DECAPOLIS

The Great Sea
Mediterranean Sea

Caesarea

Samaria

Sychar

Apollonia

Shechem

PEREA

Joppa

Ephraim

Philadelphia

Jericho

Jamnia

Emmaus

Qumran
Essene community

Mt. of Olives
Jerusalem

Bethany

Bethelhem

Hyrcania

Ascalon

JUDEA

Herodium

Gaza

Tekoa

Adora

Hebron

En-gedi

Dead Sea

IDUMEA

Masada

Raphia

Beer-sheba

Areopolis

Zoar   **NABATAEANS**

N

Introduction

In the Fullness of Time examines the early life of Christ as set against the historical background of the New Testament era. It is not only a semibiography of the life of Christ before His public ministry but also a history of the Eastern Mediterranean world at the dawn of New Testament times. Therefore, *In the Fullness of Time* will approach the life of Christ from a very different perspective.

Works about the life of Christ usually concentrate on the years of His public ministry, the last three or possibly three and one-half years of His earthly life, and say little of His early life or the historical background that surrounded it. Such works cover the events of His birth and His visit to the temple at age twelve, but other areas of His life, such as His family, His religious life, occupation, and education, remain underdeveloped in spite of biblically based information on these areas. However, the so-called "silent years" of His life, from age thirteen to around thirty, speak to us from the pages of the four Gospels.

Certainly the events of Jesus' life before His public ministry merit special study and attention. Orthodox Christian thinkers have taught that God became man. Without the incarnation, there could be no resurrection. Before entering public life, Christ fulfilled many messianic prophecies, acquired the learning and preparation for His later mission, and eventually approached the important age of thirty. Only at that age could Jewish men of the biblical era assume a public service ministry in the formal service prescribed by the Lord for Israel (Num. 4:23,47).

Nearly one billion Christians today in one way or another claim to emulate the life of Christ. No emulation of Christ's life or a study of it, however, can be complete without examining His formative years prior to His public ministry and the historical background of that era. This work attempts to fill that void in the literature of the life of Christ.

This book is written from a moderately conservative, evangelical viewpoint. I accept the four Gospels as historical literature, and I believe they provide a reliable account of the life of Jesus. Nevertheless, I recognize that there are differing textual traditions. These concerns, however, did not dampen my enthusiasm for using the Gospels as my primary source.

Other sources are helpful in filling in the Gospel narratives. These include works written in antiquity by pagan, Jewish, and early Christian authors. Knowledge of the geography of the Holy Land, archeology, and astronomy also contributes to the sum total of the information on the preministry life of Christ. Altogether, I hope this work will expand our knowledge of the most influential figure in human history.

The Time Approaches

But when the time had fully come, God sent forth his Son, born of woman, born under the law, to redeem those who were under the law (Gal. 4:4-5).

Writing years after the ascension of Christ, the apostle Paul told the followers of Christ in Galatia that God had sent His Son at the appointed time in history. While Christians since the mid-first century have regarded the birth of Christ as the primary point of reference in calculating "earth time" (B.C. or A.D.), few Gentiles or Jews who lived in the first century realized that "the fullness of the time was come" (KJV).

Gentiles in the vast Roman Empire looked to the aging Emperor Augustus to keep order and preserve the peace after years of civil war. Few of them knew very much about Judea or the Jewish faith, let alone being knowledgeable of the coming of the Messiah.

Palestinian Jews, on the other hand, longed for a Messiah. Having had to shoulder Babylonian, Persian, Greek, and then Roman occupation, through the client state governed by Herod, the Jewish people looked for some type of a Messiah to deliver them from foreign domination. The Greek word for messiah, *Christos,* was the term that Hellenist Jews used and passed into our language as *Christ.*

The Jews believed that their Scriptures, called by Christians the "Old Testament," brimmed with prophecies pertaining to a powerful and all-conquering Redeemer. They expected a semidivine Deliverer to save them from foreign oppression. Few of them had considered that God wanted to redeem His people throughout all nations—both Jewish and Gentile.

For twenty centuries Christian thought has centered on the belief that all of the Old Testament messianic promises were completed in the incarnation and mission of Jesus Christ. The Son of God took human form to reconcile a righteous God with fallen humanity. He came not only to redeem the Jewish people but also to bring salvation to the Gentiles and fulfill the divine work that they thought the Old Testament revealed only in part. Fully aware of this mission in His later public ministry, Jesus explained His role in relation to the Old Testament by saying: "Think not that I am come to destroy the law, or the prophets: I am not come to destroy, but to fulfil" (Matt. 5:17, KJV).

Indeed, the thread of prophecies and promises that were fulfilled in the incarnation and early earthly life of Jesus Christ runs throughout the Old Testament. As early as Genesis 3:15, God cursed the serpent of Eden and told him that the offspring of a woman would crush his head. Numbers 24:17 chronicles the prophecy of a star connected with the revealing of a king of Israel. God called this ruler (or Messiah) His Son in Psalm 2:7. He referred to Him as "Immanuel," or "God with us," in Isaiah 7:14 and said He would be born of a virgin. Isaiah 11:1-2 and Jeremiah 23:5-6 reveal that a descendant of David would save His people, and Micah 5:2 places His nativity or origin in Bethlehem. Even a return from Egypt for God's Son was recorded in Hosea 11:1. These passages reveal only some of the more dramatic of the nearly endless allusions to the early life of Christ in the Old Testament.

The time had arrived for these prophecies to be fulfilled. A series of events were set in motion that would produce a God-man to save His people. This history-making event did not occur in a religious and historical vacuum.

The Preincarnate Existence of Christ

Traditional orthodox Christian theology has stressed the preincarnate existence of God the Son even before He became a babe in a manger. This biblical teaching contained in John 1:1-14; 8:54-58; Hebrews 1:2; 1 John 1:1-3, and other New Testament passages is a major doctrine of the Christian faith.

Early Christians were cautioned to regard as "antichrists" those who did not recognize the Son as coming in the flesh (2 John 7-8).[1]

The preincarnate Christ, called the "Logos" (or "Word") by John in his Gospel and First Epistle, existed from the beginning of time and worked jointly with God the Father (John 1:1-2). Along with the Father, He created the universe and everything in it (v. 3; Heb. 1:2) and prepared Himself for His future redemptive work among men (John 1:9-14).

While later Christians had the advantage of proclaiming Jesus Christ as the very Son of God and the promised Messiah, the Jews of the pre-New Testament era waited and hoped for His appearance. Many became discouraged. Year after year the promised Messiah did not appear, although they never doubted that He would.

The Annunciation to Zacharias

The Gospels of Matthew and Luke record numerous instances of God revealing His plan for sending His Son into the world. Eight "annunciations" were made to individuals before and shortly after Christ's incarnation. The annunciation to Mary has received the most attention from later artists, writers, and theologians, but it was only one of these revelations.

The individuals who received these annunciations reacted in a variety of ways to these strange new tidings. Some longed for this development, while others were puzzled. Some were frightened and had to be calmed. Indeed, modern readers may feel both envy compassion for these individuals, for all of the annunciations were portrayed as either direct or indirect supernatural phenomena (see Fig. 1). They experienced the presence of God.

The first annunciation was to Zacharias, a Levite priest, at Jerusalem in Herod's renovated temple (Luke 1:5-25). Zacharias had reported with his division, Abijah, and was chosen by lot to burn incense before the Lord. The only firm time reference in this passage is that it was "In the days of Herod, king of Judea" (40-4 B.C.), and this annunciation took place late in Herod's reign (see Fig. 5).[2]

Figure 1
Eight Annunciations of the Birth of Christ

TO	BY	WHERE	REFERENCE
Zacharias	Gabriel	Jerusalem (temple)	Luke 1:19
Mary	Gabriel	Nazareth	Luke 1:26-27
Joseph	Angel (Gabriel?)	Nazareth	Matthew 1:20
Elizabeth	Holy Spirit	Judean Hills	Luke 1:41
Shepherds	Angels (Gabriel?)	Bethlehem	Luke 2:9-13
Simeon	Holy Spirit	Jerusalem (temple)	Luke 2:26-27
Anna	God	Jerusalem (temple)	Luke 2:38
Magi	Star	The East (from Judea)	Matthew 2:2

The temple duties could only be performed by the priests. As ordained in the law of Moses, all priests were chosen only from the tribe of Levi (Num. 18:1-7). The priests and Levites administered all the temple rituals connected with the Jewish faith and maintained the temple complex. King David had divided and expanded the courses of the priesthood to twenty-four (1 Chron. 24:1-19). These courses took turns in the temple service. Zacharias served in the course of Abijah, which was listed as eighth among the twenty-four divisions.

Zacharias and his wife, Elizabeth, were descended from Aaron the first high priest of Israel. For generations the business of the family of Zacharias had been special service in the house of God in Jerusalem. Therefore, the first annunciation to Zacharias, a member of the established Jewish priesthood, represented God's desire to link the advent of the Messiah to His official worship in Jerusalem. Zacharias, in effect, constituted a bridge between the Old and New Testament eras.

When Zacharias went in to burn incense one day, he encountered the angel Gabriel. Zacharias was both surprised and frightened when he heard the startling news. Gabriel informed him that he and Elizabeth were going to have a son in their old age. Moreover, this son, to be named John, would have the spirit and power of Elijah and would be the forerunner of the Lord Himself.

Zacharias doubted the angelic message and asked, "How shall I know this? For I am an old man, and my wife is advanced in years" (v. 18).

Frustrated by Zacharias's unbelief, Gabriel took his speaking ability away from him. Furthermore, Gabriel revealed that this condition would continue until John, the future Baptist, was born. When Zacharias left the temple in this state after having stayed for so long, the assembled crowd realized he had seen a vision. Zacharias, however, remained mute and could only reply to them by making signs.

Luke records that soon after this sobering event, Zacharias completed his service and returned home. As the angel had revealed, Elizabeth conceived and went into seclusion for five months. In contrast to her husband, she regarded this development as a divine sign and felt honored that her previously barren womb was now occupied. The forerunner to the Messiah was destined to be born in four months.

The Annunciation to Mary

This is the most dramatic and renowned of all of the annunciations. Indeed, this encounter came to be called "the annunciation." Doubting scholars and even some theologians questioned the authenticity of this event. The idea of God taking human form through a miraculous virgin birth stunned even the involved human participants at the time.

Before the annunciation to Mary took place, she was living in Nazareth and was betrothed to a Galilean carpenter by the name of Joseph. Both were descended from David, although their genealogies given in Matthew (perhaps that of Joseph) and Luke (perhaps that of Mary) clearly traced their way back to David by way of different routes.[3]

Although they were distantly related, Joseph, Mary, and their respective families had proceeded with the complicated steps leading to matrimony. In antiquity, Jewish families arranged the marriages of their children. The families of Joseph and Mary had already approved the informal engagement and binding betrothal ceremony as steps toward the final wedding service. A Jewish engagement was not considered binding and could be called off, but once the betrothal ceremony had taken place, a Jewish couple could not revoke the covenant between the two families and each other. Only death or adultery could terminate the bond.[4]

Joseph and Mary, now betrothed, awaited their upcoming marriage. In the Old Testament era, Jewish families and their betrothed children were expected to formalize the planned union within a year after the betrothal ceremony. Deuteronomy 20:7 contains the provision that a young man could be excused from serving in the army of Israel if he had been betrothed but had not yet married his fiancee. Joseph and Mary were clearly within that year and, like most young couples, eagerly approached their wedding day with hopes of a happy but conventional marriage in Nazareth.

Nazareth, the home of the couple, was not a notable town. It was little more than an agricultural village in Herodian Galilee with no known reputation for commercial, educational, or religious activity. Most of its residents probably pursued a living in farming and a few like Joseph were employed in skilled crafts (carpentry). Nazareth was near other larger towns and cities, such as Sepphoris, but Nazareth was hardly mentioned in the ancient sources outside the New Testament.

One passage in the Gospel of John even suggests that Nazareth may have possessed a bad reputation in the early New Testament era. In that Gospel the two future disciples, Philip and Nathanael, discussed the background of Jesus (1:45-46). Philip related that Jesus was ". . . of Nazareth, the son of Joseph." Nathanael, however, seemed unimpressed by Jesus' background and posed the rhetorical question, "Can anything good come out of Nazareth?"

While Joseph and Mary lived in Nazareth during this juncture of their lives, they also maintained ties to other locales in Palestine. After all, Mary's cousin Elizabeth lived in the hill country of Judea (Luke 1:39), and Joseph later stayed in his ancestral home of Bethlehem in Judea even after he had enrolled in the emperor's census (Matt. 2:1,8-9). Later, though unreliable, tradition also suggests that Mary's mother had once resided in Bethlehem. These Judean ties were strong, and it is possible that the couple's families had not lived in Nazareth for very long, although this observation cannot be proved from the Gospel record.[5]

Today Nazareth contains a largely Arabic-Christian community and is situated in northern Israel. The town claims to possess many authenic religious sites, but most of them originate long after the first century. One site with probable first-century (or earlier) identification is "Mary's (or the 'Virgin's') Well." The well in antiquity gave the village its water supply and can still be seen today.

Into this setting, Gabriel appeared to Mary (Luke 1:26-38) in the sixth month of Elizabeth's pregnancy. Gabriel attempted to calm his listener by saying, "Do not be afraid, Mary, for you have found favor with God" (v. 30). Then he told her that she would give birth to a son to be named Jesus and that He would occupy the throne of David and rule Israel forever.[6]

Although Mary expressed surprise as to how this would occur, she apparently did not convey the unbelief and doubt that Zacharias displayed during his annunciation. Continuing, Gabriel revealed that the pregnancy would result when the Holy Spirit would "overshadow" her and that the Son of God would be conceived in human form. To further alleviate Mary's concerns, Gabriel reminded her of the miracle of Elizabeth's pregnancy in her old age and closed by saying, "For with God nothing will be impossible" (v. 37).

Without any further questions, Mary accepted her very

special role. She exclaimed, "Behold, I am the handmaid of the Lord; let it be to me according to your word" (v. 38).

Accomplishing his mission, Gabriel left. Shortly after this annunciation, and perhaps immediately, the conception of Jesus took place. How this occurred biologically can never be known; nevertheless, Gabriel's revelation prepared Mary for her unusual destiny.

Some scholars and theologians have professed difficulties with the traditional view of this annunciation and the resulting virgin birth. Some have even labeled this account as an allegorical addition to Luke's Gospel by either himself or someone else. Usually this criticism has cited the impossibility of a virgin birth and the fact that only Luke recorded this incident.

Both objections can be answered when approached from a biblically based perspective. While the possibility of a virgin birth seems nonexistent, we might remember what Gabriel said to Mary, "For with God nothing will be impossible." A God of miracles can, indeed, cause a virgin to conceive and give birth.

The objection that only Luke reported this incident and perhaps simply made up the story, or a later writer injected it, remains a discussion in itself. Yes, only Luke records Mary's annunciation, but other biblical authors referred to the special and unusual circumstances of Christ and His conception. Isaiah 7:14 contains the first statement about the virgin birth and Luke's account records the fulfillment of that messianic prophecy. Matthew, while not recording the angelic visit to Mary (but citing angelic visits through dreams to Joseph and others), does refer to the virgin birth of Christ (1:18-25) and Mary's special role. Therefore, Luke's account is supported by other biblical writers in its assertion of a virgin birth announced by an angelic visitation.

The Annunciation to Joseph

Mary's special pregnancy certainly affected Joseph because when the conception of Jesus occurred Mary was betrothed to Joseph. Mary probably told Joseph about her condition, although the biblical narrative is silent about this detail. Mary, however, either hid the circumstances of her pregnancy from him, or he expressed some reluctance to believe her. Whatever the reason, he planned to divorce her quietly to avoid exposing Mary to public disgrace (Matt. 1:18-25).

Actually, Joseph only had two options, and he settled on the more humane one. A betrothal bond, considered as sacred as the marriage bond, could only be broken by a charge of adultery or by the death of one of the two participants. In some cases, however, a bill of divorce could be presented without giving a cause, and the betrothal could be severed.

Out of love for Mary, Joseph rejected the option of openly accusing her of adultery. Deuteronomy 22:23-24 gave a harsh punishment for a young betrothed virgin who engaged in sexual relations:

> If there is a betrothed virgin, and a man meets her in the city and lies with her, then you shall bring them both out to the gate of that city, and you shall stone them to death with stones, the young woman because she did not cry for help though she was in the city, and the man because he violated his neighbor's wife; so you shall purge the evil from the midst of you.

Little is actually said about how Joseph felt during this trying crisis. Joseph apparently did not want Mary stoned to death for adultery (Deut. 24:1), but neither did he seem to want to marry her. His very human qualms about his dilemma has made him a believable participant in the birth narratives of the New Testament. Too proper to marry a woman who was carrying a child that he had not fathered and too compassionate to accuse her of adultery before his community, Joseph inclined toward the option of ending the relationship by means of a quiet divorce. However, he continued to think about his plan before implementing it (Matt. 1:19-20).

Before Joseph could act, an angel of the Lord (perhaps Gabriel, although unnamed) appeared to him in a dream. The angel assured Joseph that Mary's condition was a supernatural manifestation of God's plan to save His people from their sins. He urged Joseph to take Mary into his home and give the child the name Jesus (Greek form of Joshua which means *Savior*). In addition, the angel revealed to Joseph that this fulfilled the prophecy in Isaiah 7:14 that a virgin would conceive and bear a son named Emmanuel ("God with us"). The angel left no doubt that God would dwell with man in the form of the child Mary was chosen to deliver.

When he awoke, Joseph resolved to marry Mary. This decision showed Joseph's courage and his willingness to follow God's will. He would have to put up with neighbors who would believe that he had relations with Mary before their formal wedding ceremony. In addition, he surrendered his immediate right as a husband in regard to sexual relations. The Matthew account contains the observation that he "knew her not till she had brought forth her firstborn son" (Matt. 1:25, KJV).

Following this annunciation, Joseph had other communications with the angel through dreams (2:13,19-20,22). The biblical narrative does not record why the angel encountered Mary face-to-face but chose to deal with Joseph in dreams. However, since God communicated through dreams with such Old Testament figures as Joseph and Daniel, these divine revelations to Joseph cannot be interpreted as a sign of divine disfavor. Regardless of the difference in how they received instructions from God, both Joseph and Mary seemed receptive to carrying out their chosen roles.

The Annunciation to Elizabeth

Shortly after Mary and Joseph were contacted by the angel of the Lord, Mary decided to visit Elizabeth in the hills of Judea (Luke 1:39-50). Mary and Elizabeth were kinswomen, possibly cousins. The Greek word in verse 36, *syggenis,* could be interpreted as relative or cousin, although most modern translations prefer relative over cousin.

While the two kinswomen obviously possessed close family ties, they identified with a different Israelite tribe. The Lukan account assigns Elizabeth to the tribe of Levi and specifically states that she "was of the daughters of Aaron" (1:5, KJV). On the other hand, Mary must have been descended from David, of the tribe of Judah, in order to bear the promised Messiah (Jer. 23:5-6). Furthermore, she married a fellow Jewish tribesman, Joseph, who was also of Davidic ancestry (Matt. 1:16; Luke 1:27). One or both of the women must have possessed forebears who married into the other's tribe. After the Babylonian captivity, tribal identification lessened among the Israelite tribes, and cross-tribal marriages increased significantly.

Mary visited Elizabeth in an unnamed town somewhere in the hills of Judea, far to the south of Jerusalem in some of the most rugged parts of Palestine. In the next few years Mary would learn much about traveling as she sojourned to places like Bethlehem, Egypt, and back to Nazareth, but this trip took her to a familiar place where her kinfolk lived. Some have suggested that the city of Elizabeth might have been Hebron. This city had been chosen by lot in the days of Joshua as a Levite city specifically inhabited by the descendants of Aaron (Josh. 21:9-13). With their Aaronic ancestry, Zacharias and Elizabeth may have lived in this city which was traditionally associated with their family and was still relatively prominent in the New Testament era.

The connection between these two kinswomen, and especially Mary's link to her relatives in Judea, is not explained in the Gospel accounts. The bond between Elizabeth and Mary thrived in spite of the great age difference and the physical distance between them. While Mary had maintained her relationship with Elizabeth, no evidence exists that Mary's son, Jesus, ever visited His relatives in the hills of Judea. The two miracle pregnancies endeared the two women all the more to each other, but little of their relationship has been revealed to us.

Although Mary knew (by way of Gabriel) of Elizabeth's

condition prior to her visit, Elizabeth apparently did not know of Mary's special mission. In fact, Luke's narrative gives no indication that Gabriel revealed Mary's chosen role to either Zacharias or Elizabeth before Mary's visit. When Mary greeted Elizabeth, the Holy Spirit came upon Elizabeth, and the child in her womb. At that time Elizabeth received the full knowledge of their common pregnancies and John leaped in his mother's womb. Elizabeth exclaimed, "Blessed are you among women, and blessed is the fruit of your womb! And why is this granted me, that the mother of my Lord should come to me?" (1:43)

As soon as Elizabeth finished her praise of both Mary and her baby, Mary also praised the Lord. Both women accepted their destinies with enthusiasm and presented a marked contrast to the unbelief of Zacharias and the calm resolve of Joseph. Mary's visit with Elizabeth was undoubtedly a high point in the lives of both women and gave each woman the comfort and support she needed. After a three-month visit, Mary returned home.

The Birth of John the Baptist

The biblical narrative does not tell us why Mary left Elizabeth shortly before John was born. Perhaps Mary had been summoned by Joseph or her family, or she simply might have wanted to go home. Since other relatives and neighbors were available to assist Elizabeth (Luke 1:58), Mary may have decided she would be of little help if she stayed. Since most scholars have estimated Mary's age at this time to be in the midteens, she may have been viewed by Elizabeth to be a little too young for childbirth assistance.

Elizabeth gave birth to John with the help and support of neighbors and relatives (Luke 1:57-80). Eight days later, John was circumcised. The seemingly ever-present neighbors and relatives who came to share the couple's joy pressed them to name the infant after his father, Zacharias, but the old couple objected. Elizabeth, remembering that the angel Gabriel had commanded Zacharias to name the baby John, said, "Not so, he shall be called John" (v. 60).

The crowd, however, continued, saying, "There is no one among your relatives who has that name" (v. 61, NIV). Then they motioned to Zacharias to settle the conflict concerning the name of the baby.

For nine months, Zacharias could not speak because he had doubted the miraculous birth of his son. He had communicated only by writing messages, and now he was asked his preference in regard to his son's name. He requested a writing tablet. Obtaining one, he wrote, "His name is John" (v. 63). Zacharias's speech was restored, and he praised God. He became filled with the Holy Spirit and prophesied of the special mission of both his son and the coming Messiah:

> And you, child, will be called the
> prophet of the Most High;
> for you will go before the Lord
> to prepare his ways,
> to give knowledge of salvation
> to his people (vv. 76-77).

The neighbors were astonished at the events which had begun with Zacharias's temple assignment. Soon the news of these events spread throughout the hill country of Judea, and many may have wondered, *What kind of child will this be?*

That question was unanswered for some time. After his birth, John disappears from the biblical narratives for about thirty years. He reappears as John the Baptist—the adult relative or cousin of Jesus. Regarding John's life between his circumcision and his public ministry Luke informs his readers only that "the child grew and became strong in spirit, and was in the wilderness till the day of his manifestation to Israel" (1:80). Having aged parents, John was virtually destined to raise himself in the Judean desert. In his later adult years, John clothed himself in camel's hair and ate locusts and wild honey (Matt. 3:4). While he most likely had contact with some of his relatives, he appears to have remained apart from his soon-to-be-born cousin (or relative) for about three decades.

Months of Waiting in Nazareth

Between John's birth and the birth of Christ, Joseph and Mary resided in Nazareth. During this time, they could not have possibly hidden Mary's condition from the townspeople; however, they resolved to marry eventually. These six months must have severely taxed the couple both emotionally and psychologically (see Fig. 5, p. 47).

By the end of this period, all the preparations that God had foreordained for the birth of His Son were fulfilled. Joseph, the earthly father of Jesus, perhaps continued to work at his carpentry trade to provide his future family a living. Or, more than likely, he took off a year for the extended honeymoon the Mosaic law prescribed for a newlywed husband (Deut. 24:5).

Mary apparently endured a normal pregnancy in spite of its supernatural origin. Nothing in the biblical account indicates anything unusual about her term, and she probably experienced the same problems, discomforts, and pleasures that other women face during pregnancy. All of God's preparations moved toward His Son's birth. As God prepared His Son for this world, the world unknowingly was preparing for Him.

2

In the Days of Caesar Augustus

And it came to pass in those days, that there went out a decree from Caesar Augustus, that all the world should be taxed (Luke 2:1, KJV).

While Joseph and Mary awaited the imminent birth of their son Jesus, Augustus ruled the world that the child would enter—the Roman Empire. Unknown to Augustus, he was destined to play an important role in the early life of Christ and the eventual spread of Christianity. Later Christians would feel that God used Augustus to prepare the world for His Son. The world of Augustus and a gift from heaven were headed toward an inevitable meeting.

Both Jesus and Augustus, however, possessed a distinguished earthly ancestry. Jesus, descended from David through His mother Mary and by adoption through Joseph, was of royal Jewish lineage. The ancient house of David, as the Old Testament had promised, was to furnish the Messiah. Jesus constituted the fulfillment of that expectation.

On the other hand, Augustus had forebears among the Roman aristocracy, and Julius Caesar gave them senatorial status. In fact, Julius Caesar was the great-uncle of young Augustus (born as Gaius Octavius) and adopted his great-nephew as his son and heir near the end of his life. After Julius Caesar's death in 44 B.C., Octavius had his name changed to Gaius Julius Caesar Octavianus to claim Caesar's mantle. In 27 B.C. the Roman Senate voted to give Octavianus the name that he has since borne—Emperor Augustus.[1]

The similarity between Emperor Augustus and the future "King of the Jews," however, ends here. They originated from two different cultures, backgrounds, geographical locations, and sets of experiences. In addition to these differences, Augustus had reached manhood (age eighteen) at the time of Caesar's death in 44 B.C. and was nearing advanced middle age at the time of the birth of Jesus.

Augustus was destined to leave his mark on history. After the death of his great-uncle Julius, Augustus jointly governed the Roman Empire with Caesar's former right-hand man Mark Antony (Marcus Antonius). Barely tolerating each other, they eventually resorted to an armed struggle to settle who would rule the Roman world. Although Anthony allied himself with Cleopatra, the last Ptolemy of Greek-ruled Egypt, Augustus and his admiral, Marcus Agrippa, defeated them at Actium. With the suicides of Anthony and Cleopatra, Augustus became sole ruler of the empire in 31 B.C. When he reorganized the empire by 27 B.C., he received the title of emperor from the Roman senate and ruled for forty-one years (see Fig. 2).

Figure 2
The Julio-Claudian Emperors of Rome (27 B.C.-A.D. 68)

Emperor	Years of Reign
Augustus	27 B.C.-A.D. 14[a]
Tiberius	14-37[b]
Gaius (Caligula)	37-41
Claudius	41-54[c]
Nero	54-68

[a]Mentioned by name in Luke 2:1.
[b]Mentioned by name in Luke 3:1.
[c]Mentioned by name in Acts 11:28 and 18:2.

Augustus then slowly remade the Roman world of which we read in the Gospels and the Book of Acts. The Lord was born into this world. Augustus and his contemporaries, like Herod, literally rebuilt the Roman world. It was said that Augustus found the city of Rome made of brick, but by the end of his life it had become "a city of marble."

In fact, many of the cities and public structures mentioned in the New Testament were constructed during the reign of Augustus. Many of the cities visited by Paul as he traveled through Asia and Greece were established by Roman veterans of Augustus's civil wars. In existing cities Augustus built temples and shrines in his role as *pontifex maximus* (head of the state religious affairs).

Furthermore, the Herods, the rulers of Augustus's client states in Palestine, added many of the cities and public structures familiar to us through reading the Gospels. Herod the Great rebuilt Samaria, renaming it Sebastia (Greek for Augustus); created the harbor town of Caesarea; built or rebuilt the rural fortresses of Herodium, Macherus, and Masada; and rebuilt the temple in Jerusalem. His sons also contributed to this building program. Antipas founded the town of Tiberias on the Sea of Galilee and named it for Rome's second emperor. Herod Philip the Second restored the city of Bethsaida and renamed it Julia for the daughter of Augustus. He also founded Caesarea Philippi (the "Caesarea of Philip") in northeastern Palestine. Christ and His disciples came into contact with many of these locales and public buildings (see Fig. 3).[2]

In addition to being a builder, Augustus was also a strong leader who ushered into the Roman world an era of relative peace. He ended over one hundred years of civil war by his victory over Anthony and Cleopatra at Actium in 31 B.C. In his *Res Gestae* ("Acts of Augustus"), which he wrote to enumerate his accomplishments, Augustus constantly alluded to his reestablishment of relative peace. References like "I freed the seas from pirates" and "I had extinguished the flames of civil war" reveal his pride in the successful pursuit of peace and order. Indeed this celebrated *Pax Romana* (Roman peace) perhaps should be called the "Peace of Augustus."[3]

Figure 3
Six Herodian Rulers of Palestine (40 B.C.-A.D. 70)

Ruler	Title	Where	When
Herod the Great	King	All Palestine	40 B.C.-4 B.C.
Archelaus[a]	Ethnarch	Judea/Samaria	4 B.C.-A.D. 6
Herod Antipas[a]	Tetrarch	Galilee/Perea	4 B.C.-A.D. 39
Herod Philip II[a]	Tetrarch	Ituria/Traconitis	4 B.C.-A.D. 33
Herod Agrippa I[b]	King	Eventually All Palestine	37-44
Herod Agrippa II[c]	King of Chalcis	Chalcis/Galilee	50-70

[a]Sons of Herod the Great.
[b]Son of murdered Aristobulus, grandson of Herod the Great.
[c]Son of Agrippa I, great-grandson of Herod the Great.

This peace aided the ministry of Christ and the spread of Christianity in the first two centuries of the Christian era. A turbulent world would not have helped the ministry of Christ or assisted the early growth and expansion of Christianity. Augustus unknowingly brought about the two conditions which the earliest years of Christianity needed—peace and order.

To maintain this peace and order, Augustus provided the Roman world with an impressive and well-trained military machine. Roman fleets ruled the seas, and in spite of sending many legions home after Actium, Roman armies exercised control on three continents. Although Roman armies stayed out of Palestine until A.D. 6, the Herodian rulers maintained mercenaries to guard their Palestinian domains. Even though Herod the Great created havoc within his own family, he subscribed to the Augustan system of keeping order within his kingdom. In fact, Augustus encouraged Herod's rule only because he knew that Herod was capable of preserving the shaky peace in Palestine.

The Relationship Between Augustus and Herod

Shortly after the death of Julius Caesar in 44 B.C., Augustus and Caesar's general Mark Antony divided the Roman world between them. Augustus took the west while Antony received the east. Both men, along with the Roman senate, wanted someone to bring order to the strategic province of Judea. Herod seemed to be that man, and in 40 B.C. the Roman senate named Herod as the ruler in Judea. In three years Herod pacified his realm (see Fig. 3).

Herod possessed an interesting background for one chosen as "King of the Jews." Herod's father, Antipater, whose family converted to Judaism, did not have a drop of Jewish blood in his veins. Antipater was an Idumaean (called an Edomite in the Old Testament) who had been the prime minister of one of the last Maccabean rulers of Judea. Herod's mother, Cypris, was of Arabic ancestry. Although Herod personally observed much of the ritual associated with the Jewish faith, he remained thoroughly Greco-Roman in his political, social, and cultural outlook.

In spite of his Greco-Roman proclivities, Herod brought order to the kingdom of the Jews. Herod's rule, however, depended on the good graces of the Roman overlords. He developed the knack of backing the right Roman master at the right time. While Antony and Cleopatra held sway over the east before Actium, Herod tended to be pro-Antony. After Actium, Herod transferred his allegiance to Augustus, and Augustus quickly backed Herod to continue his rule of Judea. In fact, over the next few years Augustus added other frontier areas to Herod's kingdom, and the two men became personal friends.

Thanks to the support of Augustus, the years between 31 B.C. to 8 B.C. were among Herod's best years. He enjoyed nearly unlimited power and immense wealth and prosperity within his kingdom. These years witnessed his expansive building program that extended beyond the boundaries of his domain. These projects included the virtual rebuilding of the temple in Jerusalem. He also kept a large standing army composed largely of foreign mercenaries to ensure his power against enemies. Herod heavily taxed his subjects to maintain an army, building projects, and his extravagant way of living, but few dared to interfere with his interests. Even Augustus refused to intervene in the affairs of Herod, for he genuinely liked him and desired his continuing rule over Palestine.

After years of uninterrupted friendship, however, two issues severely strained their personal and political relationship. These difficulties developed late in Herod's reign. The first issue was Herod's dealings with his own family. Herod married ten women and produced fifteen children. Needless to say, intrafamily rivalries and concerns for the royal succession ripped the family apart. The historian Josephus commented on Herod's family strife by saying, "For all his public successes, fortune made Herod pay a terrible price in his own house."[4]

Believing that his many wives and sons were conspiring against him, Herod frequently changed wills, imprisoned or exiled some of his sons, and eventually resorted to murder. The grisly death toll included his wife Mariamne and his sons Alexander, Aristobulus, and Antipater. Needing the permission of Augustus to carry out these death sentences, he bombarded the emperor with pleas. Augustus finally granted Herod's requests to administer the death sentences, and the sentence on Antipater took place only five days before Herod's own death.[5]

While the emperor publicly supported his old friend, he privately grieved over the fate of Herod's sons. He recommended other options besides death for all three sons and expressed much sympathy for Alexander and Aristobulus. Augustus even allowed Herod Agrippa I, the son of the murdered Aristobulus, to visit with the imperial family for a time. Making a sarcastic reference to Herod's lukewarm Judaism that forbade the eating of pork, Augustus supposedly quipped, "I would rather be Herod's pig than Herod's son."[6]

In addition to Herodian intrafamily strife, however, another issue more seriously strained the relationship of Augustus and Herod. Shortly before Augustus decided to order an empire-wide census in 8 B.C., Herod clashed with Arab neighbors over territory and the punishment of some robbers in the northeast portion of his kingdom. Herod's soldiers ravaged some of the territory of the Arabs much to the displeasure of Augustus. Angered by an inaccurate report sent to him by the Arabs, the emperor wrote Herod a harsh letter. In the letter Augustus rebuked Herod and told him that he regarded Herod as more of a subject than as a friend. While the two later reconciled, Augustus thought less of Herod and refused to expand Herod's kingdom at the expense of the Arabs due to Herod's age and the ill state of his relations with his remaining sons.[7]

Against the background of the strained relationship with Herod, Augustus ordered preparations for an upcoming census. The census of 8 B.C., mentioned in Luke 2:1-3 as the census associated with the birth of Christ, apparently included the client state of Judea, ruled by Herod.

While client states tended not to be subject to direct Roman registration and taxation, it occurred in some instances. Augustus's stepson, Emperor Tiberius, later ordered the client state of Cappadocia to submit to a census in A.D. 36.[8]

After Augustus changed Herod's status from friend to subject, the emperor probably placed Herod's kingdom in the list of areas subject to the Roman registration, as the Luke account reveals. Augustus may have even found this arrangement helpful since Herod's men had the charge of actually enrolling people for the census. The Roman officials would not have to deal directly with the Jews.

The Census of Augustus and the Birth of Christ

The census of Augustus in 8 B.C. has the only possible claim to being the registration in Luke 2. Augustus's other two empire-wide registrations were either too early or too late to agree with other chronological clues found in the Gospels. His census of 28 B.C. was too early to agree with Luke 3:23

(Jesus "about" thirty at the onset of His public ministry) and Luke 3:1-2 (this time largely being when Tiberius Caesar was in the fifteenth year of his reign—A.D. 28/29), and his census of A.D. 14 was too late (see Fig. 4).

Augustus took great pride in his censuses and listed them as eighth among his achievements as emperor in the *Res Gestae*. A Roman census entailed numerous purposes. It gave the number of Roman citizens during any registration period, furnished a list of potential manpower for military service, and provided a basis for determining taxation. The only information about this census mentioned by Augustus, however, was his observation that: "In this lustrum 4,233,000 [obviously rounded off] Roman citizens were entered on the census roll."[9]

In addition to the *Res Gestae*, the only other major source of information about this census is found in Luke 2:1-4.

> In those days a decree went out from Caesar Augustus that all the world should be enrolled. This was the first enrollment, when Quirinius was governor of Syria. And all went to be enrolled, each to his own city. And Joseph also went up from Galilee, from the city of Nazareth, to Judea, to the city of David, which is called Bethlehem, because he was of the house and lineage of David.

Figure 4
Censuses of Augustus

Year	Total of Roman Citizens
28 B.C.	4,063,000
8 B.C. (Birth of Christ census)	4,233,000
A.D. 14	4,937,000

Source: Augustus. *Res Gestae*, 8.

Critics of the Lukan account of the census tend to have three objections. First is the fact that Herod actually governed Palestine at that time, which has been dealt with in some detail. The second objection is that Saturninus, not Quirinius ("Cyrenius," KJV), governed Syria (9-7 B.C.) and that Luke confused Augustus's census with the provincial census Quirinius oversaw in A.D. 6-7 after Herod's son Archelaus had been deposed. Finally, critics have felt that the Romans never ordered people to return to their ancestral homes or birthplace for a census.

The role of Quirinius (Publicus Sulpicius Quirinius) has remained the most controversial objection. According to Josephus, Quirinius governed Syria from A.D. 6-9, but that historian wrote nothing about an earlier Syrian governorship for the Roman patrician. Yet in Acts 5:37, Luke mentioned a later census directed by Quirinius in post-Archelaus Roman-ruled Judea. This provincial census, however, could not have possibly been the census of Luke 2 since it took place long after the death of Herod the Great and wreaks havoc with other chronological clues supplied by the Gospels.

Did Quirinius govern Syria at an earlier time and oversee another census enrollment? The answer to this question has posed some difficulties to Christian scholars in light of the silence of Josephus on an earlier census connected with Quirinius. Other sources, however, have furnished enough evidence to answer in the affirmative.

In addition to Josephus, who recorded Quirinius's governorship of Syria from A.D. 6-9, the Roman historian Tacitus included a summary of part of the political and military career of Quirinius in his work *The Annals*. Quirinius was a consul with Augustus in 12 B.C. Afterward he faithfully served Augustus as a "Middle East troubleshooter." These eastern assignments included suppressing the Homonadenses in Cilicia, helping Gaius Caesar (grandson of Augustus) reorganize Armenia, and engaging the future emperor Tiberius in talks on the island of Rhodes. All of these tasks were carried out in the vicinity of Syria, and Quirinius may have been regarded as a special ruler *(hegemon)* over eastern affairs for the emperor.[10]

It is highly significant that Luke calls Quirinius a *hegemon* (2:2). This Greek word can be translated "governor" or "ruler." Luke gave Pilate this same title (3:1). In ancient literature this Greek word was used to denote the various Latin titles for Roman governors, such as procurator, prefect, and proconsul. *Hegemon,* however, could possess a more general meaning and does not have to denote a specific office. This word also was used in such Greek New Testament passages as Mark 13:9 and Luke 21:12. Therefore, Quirinius's first Syrian assignment prior to the birth of Christ may have not involved a formal specific office. In fact, Quirinius as a *hegemon* in Syria had to overlap the formal assignments of at least two governors (also called *hegemons* by Josephus) of Syria: Sentius Saturninus (9-7 B.C.) and Quinctilius Varus (7-4 B.C.) who were the formal governors of Syria during the era in which Christ entered the world. Quirinius, however, in his role as a Middle East overseer *(hegemon)* had a record of ruling jointly or in conjunction with others. After all, he was appointed as one of the two consuls along with Augustus in 12 B.C. Also, after that time Quirinius had suppressed the Homonadenses of Cilicia and Galatia in the vicinity of Psidian Antioch, and held the office of "duumvir" of that city along with an unnamed man. An inscription found there on a statue base relates, "P. Sulpici Quirini[us]—duumv[iri]." Quirinius's eastern duties almost invariably linked him with other Roman representatives of the emperor in the region.[11]

Two other inscriptions concerning Quirinius place him in Syria proper. One reveals that Quirinius was a legate (official representative of the emperor) in that province, while another inscription leaves him unnamed but clearly states that this official was "twice" governor of Syria and Phoenicia. This latter inscription can be about none other than Quirinius as the material found in it clearly matches other recorded material on him found in other inscriptions and *The Annals* of Tacitus. Therefore, Quirinius had "governed"

Syria earlier than A.D. 6-9 as an official representative of the emperor around the time of the census of 8 B.C.[12]

In light of these inscriptions and evidence furnished by Tacitus, little reason remains to doubt Luke's information on Quirinius governing Syria at the time of the census. As the emperor's special eastern envoy, Quirinius could have had a special role in carrying out the census in the eastern provinces along with the actual governors of those provinces in the years 8-7 B.C.

The last objection to Luke's account of the census of Augustus, that a Roman census never required individuals or a family to return to an ancestral home or a birthplace to be registered, also deserves discussion. For years scholars and historians thought that Luke erred in his account when he stated that Joseph and Mary traveled to Bethlehem to register for the emperor's census. They regarded Nazareth, the residence of Joseph and Mary, as the proper location for the enrollment. A papyrus scroll discovered in Egypt, however, reinforces the Luke account for the circumstances behind the birth of Christ. In A.D. 104 the Egyptian prefect Gaius Vibius Maximus ordered the Egyptian population to return to their previous residences to participate in a provincial census enrollment. The scroll reads:

> Gaius Vibius Maximus, Prefect of Egypt says: "The enrollment by household at hand, it is necessary to notify all who for any cause soever are outside their nomes [districts] to return to their domestic hearths, that they may also accomplish the customary dispensation of enrollment and continue steadfastly in the husbandry that belongeth to them."[13]

Again the world was preparing itself for the arrival of its Savior. Unknowingly, Augustus, Herod, and Quirinius provided the reason for the Christ child to be born in Bethlehem and fulfill the prophecy found in Micah 5:2 concerning the origin of the Messiah. Ordered by the emperor to return to his town of origin, Joseph and Mary proceeded to Bethlehem.

Matthew and Luke specifically mentioned the messianic town of Bethlehem as the fulfillment of Micah's prophecy.

As Joseph and Mary traveled to Bethlehem, they realized they had removed themselves from the talk and gossip concerning Mary's condition in Nazareth. Mary was not required to accompany her husband to Bethlehem for the enrollment, but Joseph took her with him. The emperor's census actually provided a practical solution for getting away from townspeople who were not so inclined to believe that her pregnancy was divine. So Augustus again played his role. He not only sent the future Messiah to His appointed birthplace but also aided the removal of Joseph and Mary from the increasing ridicule of small-town society generated by Mary's advancing condition.

Overall, the influence of Augustus and other important political contemporaries like Quirinius and Herod on the life of Jesus and His future movement cannot be overlooked. The Gospels, Acts, the Epistles, and Revelation that make up the New Testament continually allude to the political, economic, religious, social, and cultural impact brought about by Augustus, his friends, and his successors. The lives of the Roman emperor and the soon-to-be-born Messiah were tied to each other, even though the emperor himself was not aware of the link. The Roman historian Suetonius in his *Life of Augustus* recorded that some months before the birth of Augustus a prophecy was current in Rome that nature was making ready to provide a king. The world was making ready to receive a king, but it would not be Augustus.[14]

3

The Birth of Jesus

So it was, that, while they were there [Bethlehem], the days were accomplished that she should be delivered. And she brought forth her firstborn son, and wrapped him in swaddling clothes, and laid him in a manger, because there was no room for them in the inn (Luke 2:6-7, KJV).

The town of Bethlehem, located a few miles south of Jerusalem, abounds in the symbols and lore of the long-awaited Messiah. Both Jewish and Christian literature link the community to the Messiah. As previously stated, Micah 5:2 placed Bethlehem foremost among the cities of Israel since God ordained it to be the birthplace of the Messiah. *Bethlehem* in Hebrew means "house of bread," and Jesus later gave Himself the messianic title "the bread of life" (John 6:35,48).

In spite of its messianic importance to both Jews and Christians today, Bethlehem, like Nazareth, has few authenic sites that have survived from antiquity. The city in Old Testament times possessed a famed well near the city gate. King David once desired a drink from the well during one of his military campaigns and this utterance resulted in three of his men breaking through Philistine lines to bring him some of the highly valued water (2 Sam. 23:14-17). One thousand years later one of his Bethlehem-born descendants would offer "living water" to a Samaritan woman at another well in Palestine (John 4:10).

Bethlehem, the home city of David and the birthplace of Christ, even today preserves the aura of what it has always been—a large village. Although the city is inhabited by thousands today, both pilgrims and tourists come away with an impression of quaintness and a pastoral atmosphere in spite of the holiday crowds and bustling activity in the merchant shops of the town.

Around two thousand years ago Bethlehem's villagelike atmosphere was disrupted by another crowd—former Bethle-hemites returning for the emperor's census. In addition to Joseph and Mary, many other former residents with their families and kinfolk sought the town's limited lodging facilities. Perhaps some were descended from David like the holy couple, for they could have numbered in the hundreds or even thousands by the time of the imperial census. The town's inns most certainly were hopelessly overcrowded.

Inns in antiquity tended to be of two types. An inn could have been a dwelling or dwellings operated by a manager or owner who provided guests with food and lodging much like inns, motels, and hotels today. Needless to say, the services offered by these inns varied. Such inns might have functioned as the owner's main source of income.

On the other hand, an inn could have been only a room or two attached to or near a private residence. The owner only provided this service to supplement his income and was likely to be employed in some other occupation for his main source of income. This attached room may have also functioned as a guest room for visiting family members and friends, so they received first priority over any other travelers. More than likely, Bethlehem's inns tended to be of this type, and they were crowded with kinfolk, friends, and previously arrived travelers who were fortunate enough to have some tie to the owner. When Joseph and Mary reached the town, no lodging was available for the parents of Jesus in any type of inn.

Stories of the arrival of Jesus and Mary in Bethlehem often have them entering the town just before sunset or even during the night. This detail appears as an attempt to explain why they could not find lodging in the city. The implication is that others who arrived earlier in the day took the existing accommodations. Actually, the Luke narrative never reveals the time of day the couple reached Bethlehem. The time of day may not have been a factor. So many people coming from all over Palestine would have strained the limited inn space during all hours of the day.[1]

Christian traditions concerning the innkeeper who turned away Joseph and Mary have abounded for centuries, in spite of the fact that he or she (or both) were never directly mentioned in biblical narrative. Sometimes he has been portrayed as an unsympathetic man who gruffly told the couple, "No vacancy!" Most traditions, however, have painted a picture of the innkeeper as more sympathetic. While at first insisting he had no vacancies, he softened and remembered a shepherd's cavern on the outskirts of the village where the herders and some of their livestock sometimes took shelter from the weather. In some versions, the innkeeper's wife suggested the shelter after observing Mary's condition. Whatever took place and whoever recommended the cave, Joseph and Mary took up residence in the only shelter they could find.

This shepherd's cavern, now purportedly beneath the present Church of the Nativity in Bethlehem and identified as the birthplace of Jesus, possesses a fairly reliable tradition dating back to the second century. Justin Martyr, a second-century Christian resident of Palestine, recorded that Christ was born in a cavern near the outskirts of Bethlehem. While not naming the actual cave site, he wrote:

> But when the child was born in Bethlehem, since Joseph could not find lodging in that village, he took up his quarters in a certain cave near the village; and while they were there Mary brought forth the Christ and placed Him in a manger.[2]

Origen, another early church father, born in the second century, verified Justin Martyr's account of the site of Jesus' birthplace in Bethlehem. In addition to confirming Justin's identification, Origen brought out more information about the birth cavern site. He stated that the manger still existed in the cave in his day and that even the enemies of the Christian faith in the Bethlehem area acknowledged that Jesus was indeed born in the cavern.

> There is shown at Bethlehem the cave where He was born, and the manger in the cave where he was wrapped in swad-

dling clothes. And this site is greatly talked of in surrounding places, even among the enemies of the faith, it being said, "that in this cave was born that Jesus who is worshipped and reverenced by the Christians."[3]

The actual cavern identification perhaps also occurred in the second century. After the Jewish revolt in the A.D. 130s failed, Hadrian, the Roman emperor (117-138), initiated a policy of de-Judaization of Judea. He renamed the country Palestine, forbade the Jews to enter Jerusalem, and built or dedicated pagan shrines at the purported locations of the crucifixion, resurrection, and birthplace of Christ. A pagan grove dedicated to the god Adonis near Bethlehem (today in Bethlehem) actually enabled future generations to identify the site of the birthplace of Christ as supposed in the second century, even though it had been Hadrian's intention to obliterate the memory of what the location represented.

Arriving at the grotto, Joseph and Mary took up residence and awaited the birth of Jesus. The cavern provided much-needed shelter, but the facilities were primitive compared to modern standards. Such grottoes largely functioned as temporary shelters for shepherds and their animals. Since herding paraphernalia such as feed (hay and/or grain), a manger or mangers of stone, and perhaps woolen shepherds' cloaks (for cold or rainy evenings) were often found in these caves, this particular cavern seemed more like a stable than a grotto, and after that time the legend grew that Christ entered this world in a stable. These grottos, however, did not for the most part function as permanent stables.

Sometime during their stay in the cave (the biblical account does not reveal how long they resided there before Christ was born), Mary gave birth to Jesus (Luke 2:7). Wrapping Him in the binding ("swaddling") cloths that the custom of the day dictated for small infants, she laid him in one of the stone mangers in the grotto. While few mothers today would place their newly born children in an abandoned feeding trough, Mary simply made use of the best facilities available.

Mary's use of the binding cloths and a manger for her son's

needs has puzzled modern readers of Luke's birth account. Binding cloths were simply strips of cloth bound tightly around the infants of antiquity. Jews and other people of that era believed the cloths promoted strong limbs and supported a baby's back. Before the child was swaddled with the cloths, he or she was usually washed in water and rubbed with salt. The baby wrapped in binding cloths looked much like a small but living mummy. Ezekiel, the Old Testament prophet, once alluded to this postnatal procedure when he wrote: "As for your birth, on the day you were born your navel string was not cut, nor were you washed in water to cleanse you; nor rubbed with salt, nor swathed with bands" (Ezek. 16:4).

Unable to find a suitable conventional resting place for Jesus, Mary used a manger for a cradle. Although modern nativity scenes often feature a wooden manger, ancient Palestinian feeding troughs were made from stone. Hand-carved stone mangers have been unearthed at Megiddo and other places in Palestine. More than likely, the Bethlehem grotto probably contained a stone manger, and early representations of the Nativity in art showed stone mangers.

Otherwise, we possess little reliable information on the actual birth of Jesus. We do not know if a midwife was present or even if Joseph, although this is unlikely, assisted with the delivery. The delivery itself went smoothly for we read in the biblical narrative that Mary possessed the strength to bind Him in cloth, pick up the baby, and place Him in a manger on her own. While later tradition filled the grotto with many varieties of animals, the biblical account is silent on this score. A modern birth certificate contains more information on a newly born infant than we have about the birth of Jesus. Joseph and Mary were grateful that all had gone smoothly and later saw little need of sharing information about the birth with others.[4]

Annunciation to the Shepherds

The holy family received two sets of visitors while they sojourned in Bethlehem. These visitors, the shepherds and later the Magi (or traditionally the "wise men"), like earlier figures in the birth narratives, received apparent supernatural or semisupernatural indications of the birth of Christ. While the Magi represented the annunciation to the Gentiles, the annunciation to the shepherds symbolized God's revelation to the common people of Israel.

The angelic announcement to the shepherds of Bethlehem was the first annunciation to people not directly related to the earthly family of Jesus. Zacharias, Elizabeth, Mary, and Joseph all had ties of kinship to the newborn babe. However, at Jesus' birth, God ordained a revelation to representatives of His own people.

Initially, shepherds may appear to be the least likely candidates for a divine annunciation, for many aspects of sheep herding in antiquity required these men to routinely break or disregard the law of Moses. For instance, looking after sheep tended to cause them to break the sabbath when they had to hunt for unaccounted strays. Since they sometimes slaughtered animals or had to dispose of those who died in some way, they were regarded as ceremonially unclean for some Jewish rites and observances.

Nevertheless, shepherds were highly honored in the pages of the Old Testament. Virtually all the patriarchs followed this occupation, including Abraham, Isaac, Jacob (Israel), and the children of Jacob. Other noted shepherds of the Old Testament include Moses, King David, and the prophet Amos. All these men were receptive to God's calling, and the shepherds of Bethlehem maintained this traditional response to divine destiny.

These specific shepherds, however, received this news largely because of the special task they had been assigned— to watch over the sheep destined for sacrifice at the temple. The Mishnah contains the observation that the sheep to be sacrificed in the temple service were quartered in Bethlehem. The shepherds of this flock, unlike other shepherds in nonbiblical Jewish literature who had the reputation for laxity in matters of the law, anxiously awaited the return of the

Messiah like other zealous followers of the Jewish faith. Since they were guarding the sacrificial lambs earmarked for sacrifice in the name of God, they would have been receptive to hearing the good news that the "Lamb of God" had arrived to live among them.[5]

The revelation to the shepherds (Luke 2:8-20) came while they kept watch over their flock at night. The shepherds probably were in fields near the cavern. As they tended their duties, their peaceful evening was shattered by an angelic visitation. An angel, perhaps Gabriel (the angel is not named in this passage), appeared in a great burst of light and frightened the shepherds.

The angel saw the shepherds' fears and said:

> Be not afraid; for behold, I bring you good news of a great joy which will come to all the people. For to you is born this day in the city of David a Savior, who is Christ the Lord. And this will be a sign for you: you will find a babe wrapped in swaddling cloths and lying in a manger (Luke 2:10-12).

No sooner had the angel spoken these words than he was joined by a heavenly host who praised God. In unison they exclaimed, "Glory to God in the highest, and on earth peace, good will toward men" (v. 14, KJV).

After observing the angels return to heaven, the shepherds left their flock and hurried to the nearby grotto. As the angel had informed them, they found the child in the manger. They stayed and worshiped the Christ child. Eventually they returned to their duties, but recounted their experience to others in that vicinity until the news became widely known in the Bethlehem area (Luke 2:17-18,20).

In contrast to the bewildered shepherds, however, Mary chose to keep the events of that night to herself (v. 19). Deciding to let others tell the "good news" on this occasion and at other times, she prepared herself for the task of being a wife and mother (v. 51). She apparently had committed herself to providing her son with a childhood like other children and wished to forego any unnecessary excitement. With the departure of the shepherds, she simply returned to her new-found maternal chores.

Little else has been revealed about the circumstances and events of that night. Joseph, like Mary, may have also pondered what had occurred that evening. Although callers may have visited the holy family, reliable tradition has borne no record of any other visitors that night. Less reliable tradition, however, has provided multitudes of nocturnal sightseers and guests including assorted Eastern mystics (besides the Magi who came later), a little drummer boy, and other even more fanciful characters. Whatever else happened, eventually the excitement of the evening waned and the holy family found time for much needed rest.

When Was Christ Born?

The Year

Most writers and scholars acknowledge the difficulty of assigning a date to the birth of Christ. They usually propose an educated guess based on the few chronological clues we possess from the gospels. In truth, the actual birth date of Christ remains unknown.

The year A.D. 1 for the birth year is off by four years since Josephus recorded Herod the Great's death sometime in the early spring of 4 B.C. and both Matthew's and Luke's narratives placed the birth of Christ during Herod's reign (Matt. 2:1; Luke 1:5). So, ironically, Jesus had to be born four years before Himself (B.C. means "before Christ").[6]

This four-year displacement resulted from an error in calculation by the sixth-century Roman monk Dionysius Exiguus. Commissioned by the Byzantine emperor to convert the old Roman calendar in which time was reckoned from the founding of the city of Rome to a system which would reckon time from the birth of Christ, the monk made a rough conversion. He estimated that Jesus was born around the time of Herod's death. Knowing the year for the founding of Rome, he put the death of Herod at 753 years from Rome's founding when actually it was only 749 years. So this meant that Christ had to be born in at least 4 B.C.

Other biblical and historical clues perhaps push His birth year further into the B.C. era. Even if Herod died in 4 B.C., it is obvious that Jesus was born sometime prior to Herod's death. In Matthew 2:16-18 Herod ordered the deaths of all male children two years old and under in the Bethlehem vicinity. He reckoned this number of years from the time the Magi told him when they first saw the star in the east (v. 7). Although we cannot exactly pinpoint the sighting of the star by the Magi in the east in relation to the actual birth of Christ (their sighting may have taken place months before the actual birth), the possibility exists that Jesus could have been as old as two years at the time Herod slaughtered the innocents of Bethlehem. If so, Jesus may have been born in 6 B.C.

In fact, a birth year for Christ could be 8 or 7 B.C. After all, the order for the census of Augustus went out in 8 B.C., even though the actual registration could have taken place sometime after that. All these clues suggest a birth year for Christ sometime after the census of Augustus but before Herod's death in the early spring of 4 B.C. In other words, one could possibly choose any year in that four-year period.

One other biblical clue, however, tends to place the birth of Christ closer to 4 B.C. Luke 3:23 reveals that Jesus was "about" thirty when He began His public ministry. Prior to this verse, Luke wrote that John the Baptist began his ministry "in the fifteenth year of the reign of Tiberius Caesar" (v. 1). Since Tiberius began his reign in A.D. 14, John's ministry started in 28/29. Allowing for half a year to a year for John's independent ministry, Jesus began His ministry sometime around 29/30. If Jesus had been born in 4 B.C., that would make Him around thirty-three to thirty-four years old. Luke 3:23, however, did not say He was thirty but "about" thirty. A year or years before that, such as 8-5 B.C. tend to strain the phrase "about thirty" and fail to harmonize with Luke 3:1 and 3:23. Nevertheless, they cannot be fully ruled out either.[7]

A discussion of the "star of Bethlehem" in attempting to date the birth of Christ offers little help due to the many conflicting theories and dates proposed for the phenomenon. The "star," like the first Syrian governorship of Quirinius, cannot be firmly fixed in a chronology of the life of Christ and still leaves us with the birth year of Christ between 8 and 4 B.C. (See Fig. 5 for a proposed chronology of birth related events and chapter 5 for a discussion of the "star of Bethlehem.")

The Season and Month

Just as the birth year of Christ cannot be exactly pinpointed, the season and month also cannot be verified. December 25 as the date for the birth of Christ comes from later church tradition based on speculation about the season, month, and date for the Nativity. Others disagree with this date and propose instead an autumn or spring season for the birth of Christ. This speculation, however, seems as arbitrary as the traditional date for the birth of Jesus since the Bible fails to furnish enough evidence to confirm any of the proposed dates for the nativity of Christ.

The oldest references to a date for the nativity come from the late second century. Churchmen of the second, third, and fourth centuries proposed a wintertime birth for Jesus, although their guesses differed as to the month including November, December, and January. Hippolytus was the first churchman to endorse December 25, while Clement of Alexandria preferred November 18. Later writers like Epiphanius and others, predominantly in the East, proposed January 6. How they arrived at those dates is unclear, but the fact that they disagreed as to the month and date reveal how speculative they were, even if their guesses fell either shortly before or after the winter solstice.[8]

A wintertime nativity, however, has troubled some Christians suspicious of the traditional date. One criticism leveled

Figure 5
Proposed Chronology of Events Surrounding the Birth of Christ

Event	Time of Reference	Bible Reference
Augustus orders census	8 B.C.	Luke 2:1
Gabriel visits Zacharias*	———	Luke 1:5-25
Gabriel visits Mary	6 months later	Luke 1:26-38
Mary returns from Elizabeth	3 months later	Luke 1:56
Birth of John the Baptist	———	Luke 1:57-80
Birth of Christ	6 months later	Luke 2:1-20
Circumcision of Jesus	8th day after birth	Luke 2:21
Jesus presented in temple	32 days later	Luke 2:22-38
Journey and visits of Magi	———	Matthew 2:1-12
Flight to Egypt	———	Matthew 2:13-15
Herod slaughters innocents	2 years after Magi see star	Matthew 2:7,16-18
Herod dies	Early spring, 4 B.C.	Matthew 2:19
Return to Nazareth	———	Matthew 2:19-23

_____

*Could have occurred earlier than the census of 8 B.C., although unlikely.

at this theory is the observation that a wintertime journey would have extremely difficult for Mary, who was after all in a very advanced stage of pregnancy. Actually, a journey for a woman in her condition would be difficult in any season, whether hot or cold, wet or dry, but many Christians believe that God providentially watched over the couple until they safely reached their destination. Such divine care could have neutralized the weather factor. Besides, the weather during winter in Palestine today is variable, and sometimes even in December and January a warm, dry spell can last for days. So while a wintertime journey seems unlikely for the couple, it cannot be entirely ruled out.

Another objection by those proponents of a warm weather birth month is their interpretation of Luke 2:8. That verse reveals that the shepherds were out in the fields at night with their flock. The warm weather birth proponents point out that sheep in Palestine were usually penned up for the winter. While this tends to be the general rule, it is not universal. Some Palestinian shepherds even today graze their flocks in cold weather. Christmas broadcasts from Bethlehem in our own era often show shepherds and their flocks outside the city. Grazing on pastures is cheaper than buying feed for penned-up sheep.[9]

Ancient Jewish sources are helpful on this discussion. The Mishnah records that the sheep destined for the temple sacrifices were quartered in Bethlehem, and those flocks remained out all year long. The shepherds in the birth account of Luke were probably the shepherds who watched over those special flocks. Again, a wintertime birth for Christ cannot be ruled out and any of the four seasons and twelve months could have constituted the season and month for this special nativity.[10]

Day

Along with the year, season, and month, the actual birthday of Christ cannot be decisively proved. By the fourth century, the West advocated December 25, while the East included the nativity celebration on their Epiphany observances on January 6. These dates were determined from sources outside the New Testament since neither Matthew nor Luke revealed a specific date. A date for the nativity around the winter solstice originated either from oral sources that were passed generationally and eventually recorded, or from very early written materials that have failed to survive antiquity. Nothing in our biblical account points to December 25 or any other day for the actual birthday of Jesus.

In fact, the selection of December 25 may have simply been arbitrary and did not rest on any oral tradition or written support. A number of non-Christian holidays fell around the winter solstice and placing the birth of Christ on December 25 provided a "Christian" alternative to the Norse Yule festival, the Roman Saturnalia and Sol Invictus Day, and the Jewish Hanukkah celebration. Since many Christians of the third and fourth centuries had formerly enjoyed these wintertime festivals, church leaders solidified the faith of their recent converts by substituting a midwinter Christian festival that celebrated the birth of Christ. This pragmatic ecclesiastical move, along with some extrabiblical oral and written traditions, has accounted for our modern celebration of the nativity on December 25, but other proposed midwinter nativity days possessed traditions of their own that rivaled December 25 for a number of centuries.

Whatever the reason for our traditional celebrations of the birthday of Christ on December 25, the actual date of Christ's birth remains hidden to us. Any of the days of the year could be the day of the birth of Christ. The Gospel writers apparently thought this information unimportant and preferred instead to treat His birth and most other events of His life before age thirty as a prelude to His public ministry—the real scope of their narratives. In conclusion, sometime between 8 B.C. and late March of 4 B.C., Jesus Christ entered this world in an unknown year, season, and month and on an unknown day.

Day Two Through Day Seven

Joseph, Mary, and Jesus settled into a routine family life, at least to the extent possible under the extraordinary circumstances of the birth of Jesus. The six days before Jesus' circumcision on the eighth day are passed over in our biblical account. A few things, however, can be assumed to have happened during that time. Joseph enrolled in the census registration, Mary took care of Jesus, and unnamed visitors alerted by the shepherds (Luke 2:17-18) may have curiously strolled around the grotto of the nativity. Certainly this special birth became a topic of conversation in Bethlehem (v. 18).

Extrabiblical ancient sources provide only one piece of information on these three assumed events between day two and day seven. Justin Martyr, the second-century Christian writer, included a brief passage on the census registration of Joseph and his family. In *First Apology* he addressed a treatise defending Christianity to the Roman emperor Antonius Pius (138-161). Citing evidence that Christ actually existed and had been born in Bethlehem, he challenged the emperor to consult the imperial records of Rome for the register of the holy family:

> Now there is a village (Bethlehem) in the land of the Jews, thirty-five stadia from Jerusalem, in which Jesus Christ was born, as you can ascertain also from the registers of the taxing made under Cyrenius (Quirinius), your first procurator in Judea.[11]

If Justin Martyr's remarkable statement can be believed, the actual imperial record of the birth of Jesus in Bethlehem still existed in the middle of the second century. Tucked away in the imperial archives, the registration account of Joseph and his family would have contained a listing of Joseph, Mary, and the newborn Jesus. How this document survived Nero's fire in Rome cannot be known, but it could have provided verification of Luke's account that placed Joseph in Bethlehem for the census registration. Unfortunately it is lost to us today, for the imperial census records were destroyed sometime during antiquity.

We can only speculate about the information collected from the holy family in the census registration. Joseph and Mary would have been mentioned by name, but since Jesus was not officially named until the eighth day of His life (Luke 2:21), He may have been recorded as an unnamed infant. On the other hand, the couple might have given His name to the census taker since Mary had been commanded by Gabriel to name the baby Jesus (Luke 1:31). Joseph also had received the same command (Matt. 1:21). The holy family would have been classified as non-Roman citizens and, therefore, subject to providing some form of tribute. Joseph, a carpenter of limited means at this time, however, would have been assessed accordingly.

With the registration behind them, Joseph and Mary knew that the circumcision of Jesus and His presentation in the temple awaited them. They must have been a little apprehensive about the uncertain events of the near future. They, nevertheless, continued to trust God, for the promised Nativity had become a reality.

4

Circumcision of Jesus and Presentation in the Temple

And at the end of eight days, when he was circumcised, he was called Jesus, the name given by the angel before he was conceived in the womb.

And when the time came for their purification according to the law of Moses, they brought him up to Jerusalem to present him to the Lord (Luke 2:21-22).

Jesus' circumcision and naming occurred on the eighth day of His life. Circumcision, the removal of a part of the foreskin, was required as part of the Jewish faith. This commandment was first given to Abraham (Gen. 17:10-13), and every generation of Hebrews after that received their mark of identity with the nation and the laws of God.

In addition to the Scripture in Genesis, Leviticus 12:1-3 reveals this information concerning circumcision:

The Lord said to Moses, "Say to the people of Israel, If a woman conceives, and bears a male child, then she shall be unclean seven days; as at the time of her menustration, she shall be unclean. And on the eighth day the flesh of his foreskin shall be circumcised."

At this time Jesus also received His name. The name Jesus, the Greek form of the Hebrew word *Joshua* (or *Yeshua*), means "Savior." This was the name that Gabriel had earlier revealed to Mary as the child's proper name. Obedient to God's messenger, Joseph and Mary gave Jesus that name on the day of His circumcision. While circumcision symbolically linked the child to His people, His naming fixed His individuality among His people. From that day, the Son of God possessed a human name—Jesus.[1]

The custom of naming a Jewish child on His circumcision

day apparently goes back to Abraham. When God changed Abram's name to Abraham, He made circumcision a symbol of the covenant between Himself and Abraham and his descendants (Gen. 17:4-9). Later generations of Jewish families maintained the custom of naming male children on that day, although they were not specifically commanded to do so. Joseph and Mary kept this tradition as well.

On days nine through thirty-nine, the Bible furnishes little direct information about Jesus and His parents. They remained in Bethlehem, with both mother and child gaining strength. Near the end of this period Joseph began making preparations for their trip to Jerusalem for the presentation of offerings connected with Mary's purification. Once these preparations were completed, the family made the first of many journeys they would take during the infancy and early childhood of Jesus (see Fig. 6 for the early journeys and travels of Jesus).

Travel preparations in antiquity tended to be rather simple. Most common people traveled on foot. The expression "a day's journey" (Luke 2:44) meant the distance a party covered on foot during the daylight hours. This distance usually varied depending on the length of day, the size of the party (more people slowed the pace), and the health and age of the individuals involved. Therefore, the range of "a day's journey" fell anywhere from ten to possibly as many as thirty miles. Some of the common people also used a donkey for travel, but this animal more often was pressed into service as a beast of burden, carrying provisions, rather than a mode of transportation. With few exceptions, only the well-to-do employed horses or camels as a means of travel.

More than likely, the couple gathered up their provisions (food, clothing, etc.) in a bundle and set off on foot. Joseph either carried the bundle himself or tied it to a donkey if they had one. While tradition has assigned a donkey to the holy family for their travels, the biblical account never mentions one. Even as an adult, Jesus usually conducted His ministry on foot with only one recorded donkey ride—His triumphal

Figure 6
The Early Travels of Jesus and His Family During His Infancy

From	To	Purpose	Biblical Reference
Bethlehem	Jerusalem	Purification rituals	Luke 2:22
Jerusalem	Bethlehem	Return to residence	Matthew 2:1-12[a]
Bethlehem	Egypt	Escape from Herod	Matthew 2:13-15
Egypt	Nazareth[b]	Set up new residence	Matthew 2:19-23; Luke 2:30

[a]While this return to Bethlehem was not specifically mentioned in the biblical narrative, it is obvious from the passage in Matthew that the Magi visited the holy family in Bethlehem. A visit from the Magi before the trip to the temple for the purification ritual could not have happened since the Matthew account revealed the holy family left for Egypt shortly after the departure of the Magi.

[b]Joseph apparently pondered a return to Bethlehem (Matt. 2:21-22) or some other city in Judea. Hearing of the succession of Herod's son Archelaus, however, and being warned by God in a dream to forsake Judea, Joseph continued his course all the way to Nazareth in Galilee.

entry into Jerusalem. During His first visit to Jerusalem and on future trips, Mary cared for Jesus. Under these conditions, they probably covered only a few miles a day since frequent rest stops for infant care were required. Jerusalem, however, was only about five miles from Bethlehem.

The Temple Visit in Jerusalem

The purification of a mother following childbirth required Joseph and Mary to travel to the temple in Jerusalem. Luke 2:22-38 records this visit, and this passage is the only biblical account of the temple visit, the annunciations to Simeon and Anna, and the purification sacrifices.

The purification ritual, described in the twelfth chapter of Leviticus, specified that the mother would bring her sacrifices to the temple forty days after the birth of a male child. During the forty days before her purification, she was forbidden to touch any holy thing or enter the temple (v. 4). After that time she was to present herself to the temple with a lamb for a burnt offering and a pigeon or turtledove for a sin offering. If poor or unable to bring a lamb, she could substitute a pigeon or turtledove for the burnt offering. Once the sacrifices were completed, the mother would again be clean.

When Joseph and Mary arrived at the temple with Jesus, their offering consisted of the two pigeons. This indicated they were poor at the time of the offering. While Joseph could have made at least a decent, livable income from carpentry, his not being able to work steadily because of his sojourn in Bethlehem may have caused some temporary economic hardships. From this time forth, the Gospel narratives give no other indications that Jesus and His family continued for any length of time in a state of poverty.

In addition to the purification ritual, Joseph and Mary also presented Jesus to fulfill the firstborn redemption law (Ex. 13:2,12,15; Num. 18:15-16). For five silver shekels, Jesus' parents redeemed or bought Him back from the priests of the temple. Both rituals were necessary to "fulfill the law" and were the reasons the holy family went to the temple, but further developments awaited them.

The Annunciation to Simeon

While Joseph and Mary carried out the legal responsibilities in the temple, the Holy Spirit revealed to Simeon that the infant within the temple complex was the long-awaited Messiah. The Holy Spirit had previously informed Simeon that he would see the Messiah sometime before his death. On that day Simeon received the reward of his devout and sanctified life (Luke 2:25-35).

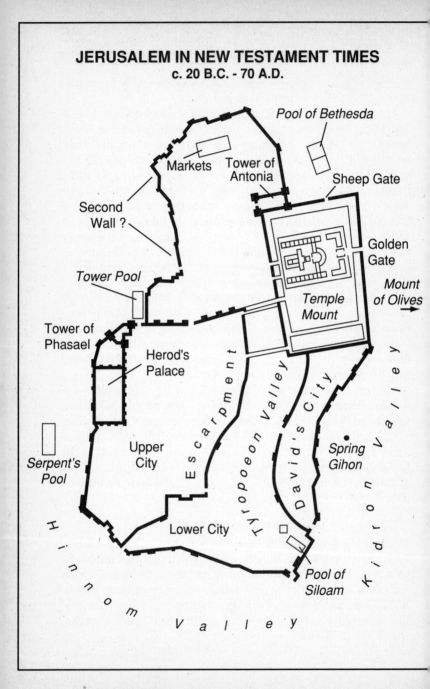

JERUSALEM IN NEW TESTAMENT TIMES
c. 20 B.C. - 70 A.D.

Pool of Bethesda

Markets

Tower of Antonia

Sheep Gate

Second Wall ?

Golden Gate

Tower Pool

Mount of Olives

Tower of Phasael

Herod's Palace

Temple Mount

Escarpment

Tyropoeon Valley

David's City

Kidron Valley

Upper City

Spring Gihon

Serpent's Pool

Lower City

Pool of Siloam

Hinnom Valley

Led by the Spirit, Simeon took the infant Jesus in his arms and blessed God, saying, "Lord, now lettest thy servant depart in peace, according to thy word: For mine eyes have seen thy salvation, Which thou hast prepared before the face of all people: A light to lighten the Gentiles, and the glory of thy people Israel" (vv. 29-32, KJV).

Although the parents of Jesus should have been used to such adoration of their child, they were astonished by Simeon's words. Knowing of their own experience with a divine annunciation, however, they recovered sufficiently enough to receive further blessing from Simeon.

Then, Simeon addressed Mary: "Behold, this child is set for the fall and rising of many in Israel, and for a sign that is spoken against (and a sword will pierce through your own soul also), that thoughts out of many hearts may be revealed" (vv. 35-36).

Speaking through the Spirit, Simeon prophesied of the mission of Jesus. The reference to "a sword shall pierce thy soul" (KJV) indicated that Mary would live to experience the agony of seeing her son die on the cross. Joseph was not given a personal message, and this perhaps alluded to the fact that he would not live to see his son's ministry and passion on the cross. Only Mary would see the mission of her son that Simeon spoke of and prophesied. Having blessed Jesus, Simeon then disappears from the biblical narrative and another annunciation occurred in the temple.

The Annunciation to Anna

Anna, like Simeon, was aged and devoted to God and longed for the Messiah (Luke 2:36-38). She was one of only a few recorded prophetesses in either the Old or New Testaments. Her father was Phanuel, and she belonged to one of the so-called "lost tribes of Israel"—Asher. Apparently some individuals from these tribes still maintained some tribal identity at the time of the birth of Christ.[2]

Luke reveals that Anna was very old. She was either

eighty-four at the time of the presentation or had been a widow for eighty-four years—the biblical Greek used by Luke has been used to support both theories. She had been married for seven years, but after the death of her husband she had entered a widowhood devoted to prayer and fasting. Regardless of the debate over Anna's age, her many years of devotion prepared her to expect the long-awaited Messiah.[3]

Rushing in at the close of Simeon's adoration, Anna thanked God for allowing her to witness her Savior. Then she spoke to those assembled and proclaimed the infant as the Redeemer of Israel. Being a prophetess, Anna said what the Holy Spirit had instructed her to say, and along with Simeon (as well as Zacharias) she provided one of the best links between the Old and New Testament eras. These two aged figures prophesied that all the old promises were to be fulfilled in due time by the forty-day-old baby before them.

Back to Bethlehem

After the dramatic visit to the temple, the holy family returned to Bethlehem. They had faithfully observed the law, and they simply desired to take up a new life in the ancestral town of both families. While they could have chosen Nazareth, they apparently wanted to live in Bethlehem for some reason left unrevealed in the Scriptures. Perhaps the stigma of Mary's pregnancy, not understood by the townspeople of Nazareth, accounted for their reluctance to return immediately to Nazareth. Their later return to that village was prompted largely out of fear of Herod's son Archelaus and a divine warning not to settle again in Judea. Bethlehem seemed to have been highly favored by Joseph in the early days of the life of his adopted son.[4]

Once they returned to Bethlehem, the parents of Jesus proceeded to establish a home. Matthew's account reveals that the holy family lived in a "house" at the time of the visit of the Magi (2:11). This piece of information, however, constitutes one of the few tidbits of knowledge we have on them during this time. Other aspects of their life in Bethlehem remain undisclosed by the biblical account, including how they supported themselves, their friendship ties in the community, and their daily routine. Nevertheless that routine was about to be broken by some unexpected guests.

5

The Visit of the Magi

Now when Jesus was born in Bethlehem of Judea in the days of Herod the king, behold, wise men from the East came to Jerusalem, saying, "Where is he who has been born king of the Jews? For we have seen his star in the East and have come to worship Him" (Matt. 2:1-2).

The Magi received the last-known annunciation associated with the birth of Christ. The visit of the Magi, recorded in Matthew 2:1-12, occurred sometime within a two-year period (v. 16). Their involvement in the early life of Jesus has remained one of the most popular chapters in His early life among both children and adults. Children know all about the "wise men" and their gifts—the forerunners of Christmas gift-giving. Around Christmas, even adult scholars have spent time in class or writing outside of class on their speculations about the Magi-linked "star of Bethlehem."

The Magi have been popular among Christians for a variety of reasons. First of all, unlike all the other people associated with the early life of Jesus, they were non-Jewish and constituted the first fulfillment of Simeon's prophecy that Jesus was "a light for revelation to the Gentiles" (Luke 2:32). Christians, overwhelmingly Gentile, identify with the Magi. The account of the Magi represented the expansion of the gospel to all people.

Second, the popularity of the Magi has been enhanced by their exotic Eastern image. Western fascination with the Magi "from the East" has endured in part because Western artists endowed them with richly embroidered Eastern clothing, stately camels, and ornate receptacles for their gifts. This Eastern addition to the life of the West's most influential personage has provided a colorful contrast to the humble shepherds and the simple common people in the early life of Christ.

Finally, the popularity of the Magi among Christians has been aided by the powerful message emitted from their brief encounter with the Lord. Although they were obviously wealthy and powerful and probably well educated (hence their traditional English title—"wise men"), they nevertheless traveled hundreds of miles to worship the divine child. The story of the Magi has illustrated to every generation of Christians that even the mighty must bow down to Jesus.

Who Were the Magi?

The popularity of the Magi persists in spite of questions about their origins and background. Centuries of myth and legend have strongly shaped our modern image of the Magi. While their number is not given in the biblical narrative, legend eventually settled on three, and even this figure has tended to be suspect since the number seemed to rest on the fact that there were three gifts. Actually logic could just have easily dictated that two Magi gave three gifts or that four, six, or twelve Magi provided three gifts. The number of gifts may not be a reliable indicator of the number of Magi.

Legend has also provided names for the Magi—Gaspar, Balthasar, and Melchoir—but these names originated long after the first century. The biblical account, as well as first- and second-century sources, gives no indication of their names.

Art often joins legend and myth to further distort our understanding of the background of the Magi. Byzantine, Western European, and even recent art works with a Magi theme often show one Magi to be a young man, another a middle-aged man, and one with a long, white beard representing an elderly man. Often they are also portrayed as each representing one of the world's major races—yellow, black, and white. These representations do not rest on any biblical or reliable literary basis from antiquity.

Even the Christmas carol "We Three Kings of Orient Are" is part of the extrabiblical additions to the Magi story. The biblical account contains no hint of their number or that they were kings or that they came from the Orient (the Far East). Legend, art, and song may actually hinder rather than help us to know something of the background of these visitors from the East.[1]

To identify the Magi, we should reexamine the biblical narrative in Matthew and other literary sources from antiquity. A clearer picture emerges, although not all questions concerning their background are fully answered.

The term *Magi* originated from Persia (modern Iran). The Magi were a caste of priests of the Zoroastrian religion of Persia. Herodotus, the Greek historian who is called the "Father of History," left an account of the Magi of the fifth century B.C. in his work *The Histories*. In addition to their priestly roles, the Magi interpreted dreams, acted as astronomers and astrologists, gave much of their time in the pursuit of knowledge, practiced magic (our words *magic* and *magician* derive from the word *Magi*), and even functioned as political advisers to kings and rulers. While their involvement in such areas as astrology and magic may seem pagan to late twentieth-century Christians, Herodotus generally credited those Magi who stayed out of politics with high moral principles. He said of the Persian customs, which the Magi encouraged:

> What they [the Persians] are forbidden to do, they are forbidden also to mention. They consider telling lies more disgraceful than anything else, and next to that, owing money. There are many reasons for their horror of debt, but the chief is their conviction that a man who owes money is bound also to tell lies.[2]

After the fifth century B.C., the Magi caste spread as far east as India and as far west as parts of Arabia. While many Magi were justly regarded as frauds and imposters, others preserved the scholarly and religious pursuits of their ancestors. The Magi in the biblical narrative were obviously upright and moral men who had studied the prophecies of the Old Testament and were wise enough to grasp the teaching that a Messiah out of Israel would bring salvation to non-Israelites like themselves. Apparently they were versed in astronomy as well as the Old Testament. Putting astronomy and the Old Testament together, they decided to undertake a journey to the land of Israel since they knew that the star they observed heralded the birth of the Jewish Messiah (Num. 24:17).

From Where Did the Magi Come and When?

The exact country of origin for the Magi who visited Christ has been long debated. Matthew's account reveals only that they came from "the East" (2:1). Historical claims have been advanced for Mesopotamia (Babylon), Arabia, and Persia as their country of origin, but none of these areas have direct biblical support.

A Mesopotamian origin for the Magi of Christ's birth has been suggested by the "star of Bethlehem." It has been thought that the stargazing of the Magi linked them to the cradle of Middle Eastern astrology—Babylon. Babylonian astronomy and astrology, virtually one and the same with astronomy to the ancients, were highly developed at this time, and the logical assumption to some scholars and historians has been to give these "visitors from the East" a Mesopotamian origin.

Other claims, however, cannot be ruled out. Arabia as the country of origin for the Magi of Matthew's account also possesses historical support. The gifts of the Magi, in particular the frankincense and myrrh, came from Arabia and were native to that area. Even gold was once plentiful in Arabia. Parts of Arabia east and south of Palestine were closer to Palestine than either Babylon or Persia, making the trip shorter than if the Magi had come from these other lands.

Justin Martyr supported Arabia as the country of origin for the Magi. His account lent powerful evidence to the Arabian origin of the Magi and predates later church fathers who argued for a Babylonian or Persian origin. He wrote: "Accordingly, the Magi from Arabia came to Bethlehem and worshipped the Child and presented him with gifts, gold and frankincense and myrrh."[3]

In this same account, Justin repeated his belief in the Arabian origin of the Magi. In one of these references, he quoted Matthew 2:18 (see also Jer. 31:15), "A voice was heard in Ramah, wailing and loud lamentation, Rachel weeping for her children; she refused to be consoled because they were no more," in regard to Herod's slaughter of the innocent children of Bethlehem after the visit of the Magi. Placing the city of Ramah in Arabia, Justin believed the voice heard in Ramah (Arabia) was that of the Magi, and after their visit wailing and weeping would come upon the place where Rachel, the wife of Jacob, was buried—Bethlehem (Gen. 35:19). While Justin's account of the Arabian origin of the Magi tends to be a little mystical, it has remained as the oldest nonbiblical account of an early church father on the place of origin of the Magi who visited Christ.[4]

Most scholars and writers who have chronicled the life of Christ, however, believe Persia has the best claim as the place of origin for the Magi. Both the word *Magi* and the priestly caste itself originated in Persia. Early Christian art portrayed them in Persian dress, and their traditional names seemingly indicate a Persian origin. Indeed the Zoroastrian Magi of Persia, who recognized a supreme God and an evil Satanlike counterpart, may have been more receptive to the monotheistic God of Israel than the polytheistic inhabitants of Mesopotamia and Arabia. After all, the Zoroastrian religion taught a belief in an afterlife, angels of light and evil demons, and a cosmic struggle between good and evil that mirrored developments in postexilic Judaism and a little later in early Christianity.

Other evidence for Persia as the homeland for the Magi has tended to be less weighty but nevertheless important. A friendship between Jews and Persians had existed since the reign of Cyrus the Great. Large communities of Jews were still in Persia at the time of the birth of Christ, and the Old Testament was no doubt available to the educated classes of

Persia, including the Magi. Even in Persia, gold, frankincense, and myrrh were traded and in good supply. Interestingly enough, the Magi could have even obtained those gifts from one of Persia's numerous Jewish merchants.

While all three areas possess some claim to being the home of the Magi, Persia seems to be the most logical. Although some difficulties arise in the choice of Persia, notably the long distance to Palestine and the lack of direct biblical allusion to a Persian origin, that country has the best claim based on other considerations and sources to being the place of origin for the Magi.

The actual time the Magi visited Jesus has posed great difficulty for those who study the life of Christ. Our only sure clue to when the visit of the Magi occurred are Matthew 2:7,16, which states that a two-year interval took place between the Magi first seeing the star in the East and Herod's slaughter of the innocents of Bethlehem. While this clue is helpful, it fails to furnish any conclusive evidence to pinpoint at what time between 8-4 B.C. that they first sighted the star in the East (at least a month or even months before their actual arrival), visited Christ at Bethlehem, and returned home before Herod's massacre of that town's infants. In addition to this, their first sighting of the star may or may not have coincided with Jesus' birth. Matthew 2:1 records only the information that the visit of the Magi took place after His birth.

To reconstruct a chronology of the trek of the Magi, we are forced to work backward. Herod died in the early spring of 4 B.C. Based on an assumption that Herod's slaughter of the innocents may have been among his last acts—and this assumption could be incorrect—the Magi first sighted the star in 6 B.C. around the time of the vernal equinox (early spring). If Herod's slaughter of the innocents took place earlier than 4 B.C., then the first sighting of the star by the Magi could even be pushed back further to 7 or 8 B.C. The two sightings of the star in the Matthew account were recorded to show fulfillment of Numbers 24:17 and to furnish the details of how the Magi were drawn to Judea, not to serve as definite chronological clues for the visit of the Magi.

The visit of the Magi to the holy family occurred after the birth of Jesus. A number of days, months or nearly two years may have elapsed between the time of the first sighting and the Magi's arrival in Bethlehem. The visit took place after the family of Joseph had returned to Bethlehem from the temple visit and reestablished their residence in that city. So the visitors from the East made actual contact with the holy family sometime after Christ was forty days old, and only then after an audience with Herod in Jerusalem. Like many other early special events in the life of Christ, the actual visitation of the Magi cannot be precisely determined.

The Star of Bethlehem

The "star of Bethlehem" drew the Magi to that city and has received much attention from both Christian and non-Christian writers and scholars. Actually the star is misnamed in a sense because its first sighting took place "in the East." We might just as easily call it the "star of the East," and other names such as the "Christmas star" and the "star of the Nativity" have been recorded in literature.

Many theories have existed concerning this star. In fact, the variety of theories has virtually assured scholars that it cannot be reliably used as a chronological clue. The supernatural star theory aids those who want to place the birth of Christ anywhere between 8 and 4 B.C. since it is not tied to any recorded natural phenomenon, but other scholars committed to finding a natural explanation of the star have advanced any number of comets, novas, and planetary conjunctions in the years 7, 6, 5, and 4 B.C. Due to the hotly contested debate on the star, a star chronology remains speculative and wedded to one of the many theories of its origin.

A Supernatural Star Theory

Some Christians today contend that the star was a supernatural phenomenon placed in the heavens by God to fulfill the prophecy found in Numbers 24:17 and to guide the Magi to Bethlehem. They reject all of the natural explanation theories and regard them as attempts to cast doubt on one of the most spectacular miracles found in the Bible.

Certainly the "star of Bethlehem" could have been a genuine miracle and may not need a further explanation. A God who made the sun stand still, turned water into wine, and calmed the storm could have placed a special star in the sky. Many Christians accept the veracity of the "miracle" of the star, and need no other explanation of the "star of Bethlehem."

Natural Theories: A Comet?

The supernatural star theory, however, does possess some drawbacks that prevent some scholars from endorsing it without reservation. First of all, it is not conclusively stated in our Bible that this was a supernatural star. Secondly, God for the most part allows the universe to run on natural law in which He remains as the all-supreme judge. The sun rises and sets, the seasons come and go as the earth revolves around the sun, and the moon goes through its twenty-nine and one-half-day cycle. The miracles of the Bible command our attention because they violate natural law. If the star was not supernatural, God could have conceivably made use of natural phenomena to produce the star.

Thirdly, the Matthew passage leaves open the possibility that the star may have been a natural phenomenon. The Greek word for star in the Matthew account, *aster,* had a more general meaning in antiquity than it does today. It was used to denote almost any heavenly phenomenon besides the sun or moon, including comets, novas, stars, and even planets. Only much later, after the writing of the New Testament, did some ancient astronomers like Ptolemy (ca. A.D. 200) make a firm distinction between fixed *asteroi* and wandering stars (*planetoi* or planets). So the Greek term *aster* in the first century covered a variety of celestial objects offered by scholars as explanations for the "star of Bethlehem."

A comet or perhaps a pair of comets may be an explanation. The two sightings of the star could have been a comet traveling toward and away from the sun and observed by the Magi on two separate occasions, or even more likely if the two sightings were months apart, they were separate comets. To the ancients a comet announced significant events in human history. A comet coincided with the death of Julius Caesar, while another comet heralded the death of Emperor Nero—or so thought the Roman historian Suetonius. A comet announcing the birth of the Messiah and the King of kings hardly seems out of place with these events.[5]

While a comet or comets offers an interesting explanation for the star, this theory lacks enough evidence from either biblical or extrabiblical sources to firmly and conclusively win out over other theories. Halley's comet, the most famous of the known comets, appeared too early to even be considered as the Nativity star (12 B.C.), but other comets have been proposed by scholars to be the "star of Bethlehem." These comets, recorded in Babylonian and Chinese chronicles, fall within the 8-4 B.C. range, but none were mentioned by Roman or Jewish historians as being visible in Palestine. Josephus reported an eclipse shortly before Herod's death and certainly would have cited a comet preceding his death, but no reference to a comet appears in his writings during this period of his account. Therefore, a comet or comets remain only one of many different natural theories for the star.

A Nova

A nova (or "new star") is actually an astronomical misnomer. Rather than being a new star, a nova is an aged star at the end of its life which has expanded to be many times brighter than its original state. If a nova explodes and throws much of its mass into interstellar space, astronomers refer to this as a supernova.

Recorded history has furnished many allusions to both novas and supernovas; twentieth-century astronomers have even photographed these phenomena. Speculation that the star of the Nativity may have been a nova or supernova has intrigued some scholars and writers, but this theory also lacks corroborating evidence in literature outside the Bible. A nova or supernova simply joins the other possibilities as an explanation for the star associated with the birth of Christ.

Planetary Conjunction Theory

Of all the natural star theories, the planetary conjunction theory remains the most fascinating. A planetary conjunction results when two or more planets line up near each other on the same celestial longitude. Since this was long before the invention of the telescope, to the ancients the planets resembled regular stars and were also referred to as *asteroi*. Proposing the "star of Bethlehem" as a planetary conjunction is, indeed, within the realm of biblical possibility, but explaining this phenomenon tends to be very complicated.

Any given planets conjoin every few hundred years. The first major scholar who proposed this as a possibility for explaining the Nativity star was the seventeenth-century German astronomer and astrologer Johannes Kepler. Around Christmas, Kepler observed that the planets Jupiter and Saturn conjoined to form what appeared to be one bright star. He then became convinced that the conjunctions of those planets might have had significance in relation to the star of the Nativity. Tracing the movement of the two planets back across time, he found three conjunctions of those planets in 7 B.C. (May, October, December) and a further conjunction of those two planets and Mars (a triple conjunction) in February 6 B.C.[6]

Kepler, however, did not report that this was the "star of Bethlehem." He regarded the conjunctions as a type of forerunner of the star, but not the actual star. Kepler's theory, however, was very popular in Bible commentaries of the nineteenth and twentieth centuries, and many Christians believe the planetary conjunctions were the actual "stars" of the biblical account. Incidentally, some use these as the dates for the departure of the Magi or for the birth of Christ, but, again, a wide variety of proposed Nativity months and even Nativity years remain as options.[7]

Moreover, the planetary conjunction theory has its problems. In none of the four conjunctions in 7-6 B.C. did the planets come close enough together to form a megastar. There was enough space between them even for the ancient observers to see with the naked eye. They would have appeared as a pair of bright stars in close proximity to each other, but not as one very bright star. In addition to this objection, observers in antiquity may have also noticed that Jupiter and Saturn traveled very close to each other throughout 7 B.C. and early 6 B.C. and may have not attached much importance to their actual conjunctions. Nevertheless, the planetary conjunction theory provides interesting commentary on the saga of the star of the birth of Jesus.

The Magi in Palestine

Drawn by the star, the Magi arrived in Jerusalem to seek the newborn Messiah. Apparently they asked many of the residents of that city an ominous question: "Where is he who has been born king of the Jews? For we have seen his star in the East, and have come to worship him" (Matt. 2:2). From this question, it was obvious to the Jerusalemites, and to us today, that the first observance of the star and the birth of the child had already occurred.

The news of these Eastern visitors and their strange mission produced concern and shock on the part of the people of Jerusalem. City residents knew Herod would not tolerate any rivals, and they feared a new round of violence from their aging and diseased monarch. Little wonder that the Bible reveals that Jerusalem "was troubled" (v. 3).

Herod also was troubled. Recently he had fought an unauthorized war with the Arabs, threatened to execute many of his sons and already had killed two, and had incurred the wrath of Emperor Augustus and temporarily lost his friendship. Now strangers were publicly announcing a new, young pretender to his throne.

Even before he met with the Magi, he gathered the chief scribes and religious leaders and asked them where the Messiah was to be born. They replied, "Bethlehem," and repeated the verse found in Micah 5:2: "But thou, Bethlehem Ephrathah, though thou be little among the thousands of Judah, yet out of thee shall he come forth unto me that is to be ruler in Israel; whose goings forth have been from of old, from everlasting" (KJV).

After hearing from the chief religious leaders, Herod dismissed them and made plans to meet with the Magi. Verse 7 reveals that he secretly summoned them to a private audience. Herod's motive was not to assist the Eastern visitors, rather to find out when the star appeared to get an idea of the age of the child so he could kill Him.

Herod met with the Magi. Ascertaining the approximate time when the Magi had first seen the star in the East, he told the Magi, "Go and search diligently for the young child [in Bethlehem], and when you have found him bring me word, that I too may come and worship him" (v. 8).

By the end of the meeting each party had achieved its objective. Herod hoped to use the Magi to find the child so that he could kill Him, and the Magi had found the town where He was located. Although the Magi seemed familiar with the Old Testament, they had overlooked the verse in Micah that revealed Bethlehem to be the town of origin for the Jewish Messiah. As the Magi took the road to Bethlehem, Herod added yet another name to his list of pretenders for his throne. He planned to wait for news about this latest pretender from the strange visitors from the East.

Meanwhile, the Magi advanced to Bethlehem. Although it was already evening, they did not wait for daylight to make the short, five- to six-mile journey. Suddenly, they noticed the reappearance of the star, and Matthew's account (vv. 9-10) records the observation that they "rejoiced exceedingly with great joy."

In fact, the star gave the appearance of guiding them to the child. It seemed to stand over the place where the infant was. They proceeded to the residence of the young Jesus.

Matthew's account reveals that the holy family lived in a "house" (v. 11). Some Bible commentators have suggested that Joseph had moved his family to a house from the cave/stable where the Lord was born. If this were so, our manger scenes revealing that the visit of the Magi took place at the stable are incorrect. Since the Greek word for house in the passage, *oikos,* does translate as house, a change of residence for the family of Joseph seems highly possible.

Justin Martyr, however, our source from the second century who identified a cave/stable as the birthplace of Christ, disagreed with this view. He placed the cave/stable as the location for the visit of the Magi. He wrote:

> But when the child was born in Bethlehem, since Joseph could not find a lodging in that village, he took up his quarters in a certain cave near the village; and while they were there Mary brought forth the Christ and placed him in a manger, and here the Magi who came from Arabia found him.[8]

Regardless of the location for the "house," the Magi entered and worshiped the child. After the long journey, they rejoiced in finding the "King of the Jews," and the residence of the child became filled with their prayers and adoration.

The Magi, however, offered more than just prayers and worship. They arrived bearing gifts for the "King of the Jews." Gift-giving for royalty was an ancient tradition. David and Solomon received gifts from subject and allied peoples and the Queen of Sheba brought gifts to Solomon on her visit to him recorded in 2 Chronicles 9:1-12. Psalm 72:10-11 reveals that the Messiah too was worthy of extensive gift-giving. The Magi bore these gifts to carry out the ancient custom of presenting worthy keepsakes to noted monarchs.

They presented Him with their gifts: gold, frankincense, and myrrh. These presents, all very expensive, were worthy of a king, for few others could afford to buy or receive them.

Gold, always a symbol of royalty and usually found among their possessions, symbolized the royal lineage of Jesus stretching all the way back to David.

Frankincense and myrrh, two resins obtained from trees in South Arabia and the horn of East Africa, are frequently mentioned in the literature of antiquity. The author of the Song of Solomon recorded the lovers comparing each other to the fragrant incenses, and 2 Chronicles 9:1-12 reveals that the Queen of Sheba (a kingdom in Southern Arabia) brought these "spices" to King Solomon in Jerusalem. The Greek historian Herodotus believed an Arab story that "flying snakes" guarded the frankincense trees of Arabia. These aromatic resins were highly prized and in much demand among those who could afford them.[9]

The two spices had numerous uses in antiquity. Frankincense *(Boswellia carterii)* was used as an incense, spice, and as an ingredient in ointments. Myrrh (from the myrrh tree, *Balsamodendronmyrrha)* had those uses as well and was also used in mouthwash, embalming, and medical formulas. Most consumers, however, used it as an incense.

Like the gold given to the Christ child, the two incenses possessed a symbolic meaning. The frankincense signified the priestly office He was to hold, for priests in the Old Testament burned frankincense during their prayers to God. Christ would be the priest-like intercessor between humans and God.

Myrrh was used in burial ointments and oils. Myrrh and death became linked through this practice. Little wonder that the Hebrew and Arab root word for myrrh *(murr)* means "bitter." The gift alluded to the fact that the child would one day die for the sins of fallen humanity. Ironically, the Bible recorded that Jesus was buried with myrrh (John 19:39). The incense presented to Him shortly after His birth followed Him to His death.

In addition to the symbolic significance of the gifts, however, a very practical consideration of this gift-giving developed. Shortly after the Magi left, God told Joseph to take his family to Egypt. Still poor at this time, the gifts of the Magi may have furnished the means for Joseph and his family to go and live in Egypt. Although they did not know this, God used the Magi to provide the financing of His Son's journey to Egypt.

The Bible reveals that shortly after the presentation of the gifts, the Magi were warned in a dream not to return to Herod. They left Bethlehem and took an alternate route to their homeland. While their stay in Bethlehem had not been long, they achieved the purpose of their journey—the worship of the true King of the Jews.[10]

They also left an enduring cultural legacy to the Christian community. Every Christmas their story is retold and their visit commemorated. Spice cakes remind us of their spices, gifts are given to others as they gave gifts to the Christ child, and a reminder of the star they saw rests upon millions of Christmas trees. Many of our Christmas customs originated from their short visit, and their cultural impact can be expected to continue.

Even more important than their cultural impact is the fact that the Magi fulfilled the divine undertaking ordained of God. The visit of these Gentile seekers to the Jewish Messiah foreshadowed a time when millions of Gentiles would seek the King of the Jews and His rule over their lives. Their faith and determination to see the child endured in spite of their long journey, their uncertainty in locating His birthplace, and an encounter with a man who thought he was the "King of the Jews." Perhaps their faith rested in part upon reading what Isaiah the prophet had written about the child seven hundred years earlier (Isa. 9:6-7):

> For unto us a child is born, unto us a son is given: and the government shall be upon his shoulder: and His name shall be called Wonderful, Counsellor, The mighty God, The everlasting Father, The Prince of Peace. Of the increase of his government and peace there shall be no end, upon the throne of David, and over his kingdom, to order it, and to establish it

with judgment and justice from henceforth even for ever. The zeal of the Lord of hosts will perform this (KJV).

While the Magi's part in the early life of Christ was finished, their visit unleashed turmoil in the land of Israel. That storm brought about by a brooding Herod uprooted the holy family and brought death to Bethlehem and its surrounding area. The Magi, however, were long gone by then.

6

Sojourn in Egypt

Now when they had departed, behold, an angel of the Lord appeared to Joseph in a dream and said, "Arise, take the child and his mother, and flee to Egypt, and remain there until I tell you; for Herod is about to search for the child, to destroy him" (Matt. 2:13).

Herod probably waited at most only a few days for the Magi to return to Jerusalem after their visit to the Christ child. However, the time that elapsed between the departure of the Magi and Herod's decision to slaughter the children of Bethlehem is not given in the biblical account. Given the nature of Herod's patience in his later years, it seems inconceivable that he would have waited for any long period of time. As it soon became apparent that the Magi were not returning, Herod seethed with rage and regarded this as yet another betrayal in his suspicious and nearly demented mind.

In fact, Herod was physically, emotionally, and mentally ill by this time. Around 5-4 B.C. Herod had aged beyond his years. Josephus recorded that Herod had difficulty in breathing, suffered from spasms and swelling in his feet and abdomen, ran a fever, had constant pains in his lower bowel, and had even developed gangrene in his genitals. These symptoms seem to indicate a number of possible diseases, including hardening of the arteries, numerous disorders of the cardiovascular system, cirrhosis of the liver, diabetes, and perhaps cancer. Not even the best physicians of Palestine or the hot baths at Callirhoe could heal his aged and diseased body.[1]

In addition to those physical difficulties, Herod's emotional and mental state had driven him to new depths of depravity. By this time he had murdered his wife and two sons and was plotting the death of another son. He tended to be mistrustful and paranoid, feared assassination, and kept his own family on edge by frequently changing wills and making outrageous demands of them. When two esteemed rabbis, Judas Ben-Sephoreus and Matthias Ben-Margalus, and forty of their followers took advantage of Herod's illness to cut down an idolatrous golden eagle, he arrested them. When they defended their action by quoting the law of Moses, Herod exploded in a furious tantrum, ordered the rabbis burned alive, and handed the other defendants over to his guard for execution.[2]

That was Herod's condition at the time of the visit of the Magi. Feeling cheated and betrayed by the Eastern visitors, he hatched a plan to make sure he got the child they spoke of as "King of the Jews." He decided to murder all the male children of Bethlehem who were two years old and under, for it had apparently been about two years since the Magi first saw the star in the East. Since Herod thought so little of murdering his own sons, he would think nothing of killing the sons of others.

Before this could be carried out, however, God intervened to protect Jesus and the Magi. The Magi were warned in a dream not to return to Herod and took another route back to their country of origin. In addition to this, a divine messenger appeared to Joseph in a dream and warned him of the danger posed to Jesus.

The angel told Joseph, "Rise, take the child and his mother, and flee to Egypt, and remain there until I tell you; for Herod is about to search for the child, to destroy him" (Matt. 2:13).

Joseph probably did not wait for daylight, but quickly gathered his family and fled Bethlehem for Egypt. Since Bethlehem was on one of the branch caravan routes to Egypt, he had little difficulty locating the main road to that country. Once again the family of Joseph was on the move, but this time they headed out of the land of Israel for an uncertain foreign interlude.

Egypt, however, was no stranger to wandering Israelites. Israel's grandfather Abraham sojourned in Egypt during a famine in Palestine. Israel (Jacob) and his sons fled to Egypt for the same purpose two generations later and stayed there in peace under the watchful eye of Joseph. Their descendants were eventually led back to Canaan by Moses. Hundreds of years later Jewish refugees fleeing the capture of Jerusalem by the Babylonians also went to Egypt. Among them was the "weeping prophet" Jeremiah. Alexander the Great invited both Egyptian and Palestinian Jews to people his Egyptian city Alexandria. Eventually, Jews made up a large percentage of that city's population. By the time of Christ, Egypt not only remained as a refuge for fleeing Jews but also was home to a sizable Jewish population.

On the other hand, Egypt hardly possessed a perfect record in accommodating Jewish refugees. Historically the country had functioned as a center for idolatry-ridden polytheism, dictatorial rule by oppressive monarchs, and often violent anti-Semitism. The Israelites had suffered persecution at the hands of Pharaoh that was only relieved by the exodus. Joseph and Mary may have especially recalled Pharaoh's cruelty toward Israelite infants (Ex. 1:15-22). Nevertheless, they continued their journey to that country. They believed the angel's promise that Egypt would provide a refuge for their son.

Their flight to Egypt must have been a trial of faith. A couple with a small infant has little desire to tackle a journey to a foreign country under trying conditions, but they accomplished that feat. Inspired by the angel's promise of eventual rescue, the couple narrowly missed a wrathful Herod and still faced an uncertain interlude in Egypt.

The family's journey to Egypt was not chronicled by the Bible's writers. Matthew, the source of the Egyptian journey and sojourn, wrote only of the nighttime departure of the family from Bethlehem. The details of their trip to Egypt were not recorded, but reasonable speculation may help fill in some of the lacking details. The journey itself was probably financed by selling or trading the gifts of the Magi either along the way or in Egypt. Due to their hasty departure, it is doubtful that Joseph took many of his carpentry tools or if he even had any in Bethlehem; so the gifts of the Magi paid for the family's trip, as well as their stay in Egypt.

For safety they may have joined a caravan, which afforded a means of protection against robbers. In fact, later third-, fourth-, and fifth-century (unreliable sources for the early life of Jesus) works tell of an attack on the family of Joseph by robbers. The story records that one robber took pity on them and let them continue their journey. This robber, later in the story, is the repenting thief on the cross. This pious legend has little value as a historical source, but it points out the dangers of desert traveling. To avoid these dangers, Joseph may have joined a caravan large enough to discourage an attack by robbers.[3]

One final speculation concerning their arrival in Egypt is that they chose to live among other Jews. Cities throughout Egypt had Jewish communities, especially in the delta region of northern Egypt. Being devout Jews, they naturally preferred to be among one of their own communities, and awaiting the angel's promised message to send word (Matt. 2:13), they probably remained near the road to Palestine. While Roman Catholic, Orthodox, and Coptic churches in Egypt today point to certain locales as being a place where the family of Joseph either stopped or lived, none of these shrines have biblical or early historical support.

Like the journey to Egypt, we possess little reliable information on the family's residence in that country. The Bible records that they remained in Egypt until the death of Herod (v. 14) and that the stay in Egypt fulfilled an Old Testament prophecy found in Hosea 11:1—"When Israel was a child, I loved him, and out of Egypt I called my son." Other than this, no other information on their sojourn in Egypt is recorded in biblical narratives.

The Slaughter of the Innocents

Meanwhile, events in Palestine were coming to a boil. Herod proceeded to carry out his plan to kill the young pretender who he thought still resided in Bethlehem. Dispatching soldiers who would do his bidding was a relatively simple task. Germanic, Thracian, and Gallic merceneries were loyal to the old tyrant. Permanent garrisons of troops close to Bethlehem resided in both Jerusalem and Herodium. The latter, a Herodian fortress in the hills above Bethlehem, may have functioned as the "base of operations" for the tragic mass murder that took place "in Bethlehem and in all that region" (Matt. 2:16).

Herod ordered his troops to kill all male children two years old and under in Bethlehem and in the vicinity around it. He arrived at this calculation based on when the Magi first observed the star in the East, for he had figured out that the first sighting may have been a premonition of the coming birth and may not have coincided with the actual birth. Therefore, Herod ordered the deaths of the males under two years old. Like Pharaoh killing the male Hebrew babies in Egypt, Herod was no respecter of human life, even of the most innocent.

The account of Herod's killing of the innocent children is derived almost exclusively from the Gospel of Matthew (vv. 16-18). Another ancient, however, alludes to the incident. Macrobius (around A.D. 400), in his work the *Saturnalia*, also referred to Herod's slaughter of the innocents. The *Saturnalia* was written as a work of fiction that the author presented in the form of dialogue set during the pagan Saturnalia festivities. In a section devoted to the wit of the emperor Augustus, the following passage was recorded: "When he [Augustus] heard that Herod King of the Jews had ordered boys in Syria under the age of two years to be put to death and that the King's son was among those killed, he said: 'I'd rather be Herod's pig than Herod's son.'"[4]

Admittedly, the validity of accepting the Macrobius passage as a legitimate non-Christian verification of Herod's crime against the children of Bethlehem seems farfetched. Macrobius lived 400 years after the birth of Christ and could have possibly read Matthew's account. Macrobius, although a non-Christian and an admirer of the pagan past, seemed familiar with the Christians and their literature. He simply could have incorporated a garbled version of Herod's mass murder of the infants in his work.

Furthermore, other problems are evident in the passage. Herod never governed Syria proper. According to Matthew's account, the killing took place only around Bethlehem and never reached Syria or other areas in Palestine. While Herod eventually murdered three of his own sons, they were all adults. He killed none in their infancy.

On the other hand, the Macrobius reference might represent an independent nonbiblical tradition of the slaughter of the innocents. Augustus may have actually said this of Herod and this version of the terrible event survived in the form that Macrobius related. Other quips attributed to Augustus in this section have been cited in other ancient sources and Macrobius hardly made those up. His references to other written works of antiquity in the *Saturnalia* abound, and many of them are lost to us today. Therefore, this version of Herod's crime possibly existed alongside the account found in the Gospel of Matthew, and only remains today because of its inclusion in the *Saturnalia*.

Overall, the *Saturnalia* passage actually confirms what Matthew wrote about the killing of the innocents. While in conflict on some points with the Matthew account, it agrees with the First Gospel that Herod murdered children up to two years old.

No reliable figure on the number of slaughtered children has ever existed, although churchmen, scholars, and writers have proposed estimates ranging from unlikely to probable. The major reason for the wide range appears to be how to interpret the geographical scope of Herod's sweep since the Matthew account has not revealed to us the exact extent of "Bethlehem and in all that region" (v. 16). Therefore, older Eastern church traditions have guessed numbers in the thousands with one Coptic Church figure topping the list with fourteen thousand.

Western speculation on the number of murdered children

has placed the figure much lower, with recent scholars proposing relatively low estimates. Paul Maier, author of *First Christmas,* wrote that the number of slaughtered children probably totaled no more than twenty-five. He arrived at this figure by confining Herod's sweep to only the village of Bethlehem, and by estimating that the village possessed about two thousand inhabitants. While Maier's calculations seem more plausible than the Eastern traditions, the actual casualty figure remains unknown.[5]

The people of Bethlehem and all the people who lived during Herod's reign had yet another reason to fear the hated tyrant. In fact, as death neared, Herod's crimes became more lurid. Egypt, indeed, offered a safe haven for Jesus and His parents.

The Death of Herod

Probably not long after the slaughter of the innocents, Herod faced the last agonizing weeks of his life. He ordered his servants to convey him to Callirhoe in Transjordan Perea where he hoped that the hot baths would help his illnesses. Although he bathed in both hot water and oil, his health did not improve, so he gave up trying to live. He commanded that part of his fortune be distributed to his loyal soldiers and asked to be returned to his living quarters at Jericho.

While at the Jericho, he hatched another diabolical mass murder. Knowing that he would die imminently, he ordered that the most important men from every village in Judea be brought to the Jericho hippodrome (race track) and be imprisoned. He sent for his sister Salome and her husband Alexas and told them:

> I know the Jews will greet my death with wild rejoicings; but I can be mourned on other people's account and make sure of a magnificent funeral if you will do as I tell you. These men under guard—as soon as I die, kill them all—let loose soldiers among them; then all Judea and every family will weep for me—they can't help it.[6]

This proposed outrage dwarfed even his slaughter of the innocents. Herod's soldiers, already being paid bounties from his estate even while he yet lived, would have carried out the order. Luckily for the proposed victims, however, Salome never gave the command for their mass execution.

Another matter shortly occupied Herod's attention. A communication arrived from the emperor that Herod had his permission to kill his son Antipater, even though the message recommended banishment if Herod was so inclined. Herod did not immediately decide to execute his son and instead took a knife with which he was cutting up an apple and attempted suicide. His cousin Achiab, however, prevented his suicide, even though loud cries in the palace gave many the impression that Herod was dead.

These rumors soon reached Antipater in jail, and he offered his jailers a bribe to let him go. The prison governor, however, not only refused it but also reported the attempted bribe to Herod. In a tantrum, Herod at once sent his bodyguards to put Antipater to death, and they quickly carried out his orders.

Nevertheless, Herod only outlived Antipater by five days. He had changed his will again and named Archelaus to be his successor and two other sons, Antipas and Herod Philip II, to govern other portions of his kingdom. He died in the spring of 4 B.C. after having reigned for thirty-six years.

The Reign of Archelaus

Salome and the king's advisers quickly worked to carry out the smooth transition of power from Herod to his sons. Salome managed to release those prisoners detained in the hippodrome, informed the soldiers of Herod's death, and ordered soldiers and civilians alike to assemble in the Jericho amphitheater for the reading of Herod's will.

At the theater Herod's will was read. Archelaus was to be king of Judea, Idumea, and Samaria. Herod Philip II received districts in northern Palestine, and Antipas inherited Galilee and Perea across the Jordan. A letter was also read to Herod's soldiers, appealing for their support for Archelaus.

Throwing their support to Archelaus, the soldiers joined him in providing for Herod's funeral. Archelaus took care of the funeral arrangements, which included a military procession to Herod's final resting place at Herodium above Bethlehem. Thracian, Germanic, and Gallic soldiers guarded the Herodian family mourners, and they were followed by the household slaves and freedmen carrying the burial spices. This procession bore Herod for twenty-four miles to Herodium. Ironically, the Bethlehem area produced and witnessed two royal events. One King was born in a cave/stable just outside of the city and received frankincense and myrrh spices to commemorate the event, while another was buried above the city at Herodium.

After Herod's burial, Archelaus awaited the decision of Augustus to confirm his kingship. He mourned for his father for a week and then went to Jerusalem for the Passover. Although Archelaus was still unconfirmed as king, the crowds (swelled by feast observers) treated him as one, and Archelaus, in turn, promised to be a better ruler than his father.

Unfortunately for Archelaus, the crowd soon demanded that he produce evidence of his good faith. They specifically asked for taxation cuts, punishment of those responsible for the deaths of the two learned rabbis, and the removal of Herod's high priest. Infuriated by the mob's arrogance, Archelaus refused to carry out their demands and ordered officers to ask the crowd to disperse. He did not want to use force, but when the mob stoned his officers, Archelaus sent in the army to clear the streets. Soldiers brutally dispersed the crowd with much loss of life and heralds announced that Herod's successor had called off the feast and ordered everyone to go home. Archelaus began his reign by killing three thousand of his subjects in a Passover massacre.

It was little wonder that God removed His Son to Egypt, for all of Palestine except Samaria soon broke out in revolt or counterrevolt. Armed mobs and Herodian soldiers swarmed to take up the cause of Archelaus or other Herodian claimants, like Antipas, or even non-Herodian claimants. Robbers and brigands plagued Galilee and Perea, and Roman soldiers fought Jewish mobs in Jerusalem. In fact, Archelaus never really brought complete order to Palestine during his approximately ten-year reign.

Augustus eventually recognized Herod's last will and confirmed the authority of Archelaus, Antipas, and Herod Philip II in their respective areas. However, the anarchy in Palestine prevented the emperor from giving Archelaus the title of king. Instead Archelaus was proclaimed ethnarch with a promise of a future royal title if he proved himself worthy.

Archelaus, however, never achieved the title, for he continued to misrule and incurred the hatred of his subjects. When embassies from both the Jews and Samaritans requested his removal, the emperor finally banished him to Gaul after a few years. Archelaus and Herod's other sons, Herod Philip II excepted, continued the sins of their father.[7]

"Out of Egypt I Called My Son"

Meanwhile, the holy family's stay in Egypt neared its end. With Herod dead and Archelaus attempting to bring order to an unconfirmed and uncertain reign, the unnamed angel (probably Gabriel) again appeared to Joseph in a dream. Joseph was told, "Rise, take the child and his mother, and go to the land of Israel, for those who sought the child's life are dead" (v. 20).

That very morning Joseph gathered his family and left Egypt. Apparently Joseph had planned to return to Bethlehem or some other city in Judea, for the angel had to warn him in yet another dream not to resettle in Judea (vv. 21-22).

Joseph, however, was beginning to have his own misgivings about living in a chaotic Judea under Archelaus. On the way back to Palestine, he must have heard of Archelaus' reign and the calamities associated with it. Therefore, he bypassed Judea and returned to Nazareth in Galilee. Here another evil son of Herod reigned. Antipas, however, was bringing order to his area with the assistance of Roman legions and foreign mercenaries. Galilee was free of insurrections for a while, and a family could be raised there in relative peace.

The decision to return to Nazareth also made sense from a pragmatic perspective. Both Joseph and Mary had lived there before and had ties to the city. Recently torn by civil strife and warfare, Galileans had enough worries of their own without having to concern themselves about Mary's strange pregnancy and the departure from Nazareth at the time of the census. In fact, the hometown crowd later found in each of the four Gospels appears not to have taunted either Jesus or His mother about the circumstances surrounding those events.

Both Matthew 2:23 and Luke 2:39 record the holy family resettling in Nazareth, but Matthew's account reveals one other curious piece of information. It says that "he [Joseph] went and dwelt in a city called Nazareth, that what was spoken by the prophets might be fulfilled, 'He [Jesus] shall be called a Nazarene'" (v. 23).

Once the family settled in Nazareth, their traveling and sojourning came to an end. The first two or three years of Jesus' life were spent in many different locales: Nazareth, Bethlehem, Jerusalem, Egypt, and back to Nazareth. A new chapter in the life of Christ was about to begin—His childhood.

7

The Childhood of Jesus

And when they had performed all things according to the law of the Lord, they returned into Galilee, to their own city, Nazareth. And the child grew and waxed strong in spirit, filled with wisdom: and grace of God was upon him (Luke 2:29-40, KJV).

The Galilee to which the holy family had returned had changed both in physical appearance and as a political unit. Whole villages and towns had been destroyed in the anarchy that followed Herod the Great's death. When a Galilean rebel named Judas Ben-Hezekiah seized the town of Sepporis and challenged the Roman army, the Romans destroyed the city and enslaved the former inhabitants.[1] Other Galilean locales had also been ravaged.

Herod's son Antipas, often called Herod the Tetrarch in the Gospel narratives, ruled Galilee as well as the Transjordan province of Perea. Antipas brought order to the province with the aid of the Romans and Herodian mercenaries; but while the area remained fairly peaceful through much of his reign, Galilee harbored strong anti-Roman and anti-Herodian sentiment that sometimes produced outbreaks of violence. The most notable of these short-lived rebellions occurred at the time of Quirinius's census of A.D. 7 and was led by Judas of Galilee mentioned in Acts 5:37 and also mentioned by Josephus. Antipas, nevertheless, held on to his tetrarchy in spite of the challenges until A.D. 39 and embarked on a rebuilding program that lasted throughout his reign. It was little wonder that Jesus called him "that fox" (Luke 13:32).[2]

The Galileans were busy with the task of reconstruction when Joseph and Mary with their child returned to Nazareth. The residents of Nazareth had experienced firsthand the ravages of war and pillage. After all, nearby Sepphoris no longer existed and many of their friends and family members had perished in the fighting or had been enslaved. While they knew Joseph and Mary, the residents of Nazareth could have hardly given them a rousing homecoming, for many of their own friends and relatives were little more than refugees who needed their help. A rebuilding Galilee took little notice of the holy family at this time. They, too, appeared to be just returning displaced persons.

While Joseph and his family put down roots in Galilee, they realized that the province was hopelessly divided along ethnic, religious, and political lines. These divisions, however, did not seem as dangerous to their well-being as living in Judea governed by Archelaus. First of all, Galilee was only half Jewish. The other half, Gentiles, were largely Greeks or Greek-speaking Syrians. In fact, both Old and New Testaments called the region "Galilee of the Gentiles" (Isa. 9:1, KJV—also quoted in Matt. 4:15). Greek and Hebrew cultures existed side by side, yet they were segregated, for many Jews desired to live apart from what they regarded as the corrupting influences of the Hellenists. Jesus grew up in a region that was just as much Hellenic as Hebrew.

Galilee also divided along religious lines. In addition to the pagan/Jewish split along the ethnic divisions, the Jews themselves parted on differences of interpretation. Influenced by Hellenist culture, upper-class Jews often fell into the Sadducee camp. Sadducees denied the existence of the resurrection, angels, and heaven and hell. They were stronger in the big cities of Galilee, and they usually supported the Jewish aristocracy, who dominated the temple worship in Jerusalem.

Supposedly, the Sadducees were the religious liberals of their day. Their admiration of Greco-Roman culture certainly influenced them toward acceptance of new ideas and a more tolerant attitude of other non-Jewish faiths. In reality, however, the Sadducees tended to be social, political, and religious conservatives who backed their conservative Roman and Herodian rulers. The Sadducees desired to follow the letter of the law of Moses without the more recent oral tradition so loved by the Pharisees. Since the law of Moses played down the afterlife, the resurrection, and angels, they regarded these as later additions to the faith that needed to be rejected.

Galilee, however, also contained the even more influential Pharisees. The Pharisees accepted the resurrection, angels, and the afterlife. The Jewish people largely looked to them for spiritual and moral leadership, and the Pharisees tended to be stronger in the small towns and villages of the region. Outside of the big cities of Galilee, they controlled the religious institutions, including the synagogues, and zealously fought the Hellenistic influences that the Sadducees had accepted. Their zeal for Jewish religious traditions not contained in the sacred writings often led to a self-righteousness that the adult Jesus challenged.

Other Jewish sects like the Essenes may have also had adherents in Galilee, but the Essenes and the Gnostic-influenced Jewish sects were far more numerous in Judea. These other religious sects, nevertheless, did have followers in the region and provided Jewish alternatives to both the Pharisees and Sadducees. This foreshadowed a time when the followers of John the Baptist and Jesus would challenge the Pharisee/Sadducee religious monopoly in the region.

Finally, Galilee divided along political lines. Most of the Jewish and Gentile upper classes supported the rule of the Herods and became known as the Herodian party. Some Greeks in Galilee may have desired the autonomous self-governing status within the Roman Empire that the Greek-speaking cities of nearby Decapolis possessed, but even they largely favored Herodian rule either by choice or by a fear of another less pro-Hellenist Jewish ruler.

Outside of the upper-class Jewish community, however, Herodian rule tended to be less popular. Many Jews considered the Herods as little more than figureheads for direct Roman rule. Some even resorted to violence to oppose Herodian and Roman rule and eventually became collectively known as the Zealots. Galilee became a stronghold of Zealot activity and required the mercenary army of Herod the Tetrarch to be on constant alert. The Zealots sometimes combined Pharisee religious values with their Jewish nationalism and also functioned as a religious movement as well. Later, even one of Jesus' disciples, Simon the Zealot (Luke 6:15; Acts 1:13), may have once been considered a member of this movement. While all of these ethnic, religious, and political divisions must have surely caused strains on the lives of the people of Galilee, Joseph and Mary, guided by their faith, decided to raise Jesus in such an environment.

Early Religious and Educational Training of Jesus

In Nazareth Joseph and Mary, for the first time in their marriage, settled down to a fairly normal routine. Joseph returned full time to his carpentry trade, while Mary kept the home and spent much time with her son. As Jesus grew, His parents must have realized that He needed to learn about His faith.

Actually, the religious and educational training of any Jewish boy in this era were one and the same. Learning the Jewish faith was an education, and education had the aim of producing a person knowledgeable in Judaism. The Book of Proverbs revealed to Jewish parents that the respect due to God was the basis of all education. Proverbs 1:7 reminded them that "the fear of the Lord is the beginning of knowledge; but fools despise wisdom and instruction."

Proverbs 1:8; 6:20; and 10:1 underscore the point that religious and educational instruction were considered to be the collective responsibility of both parents, even though the bulk of the Book of Proverbs appears to be in the form of a father's instruction to his son. While both parents had the responsibility, the father ultimately had to answer for his son's religious education. No doubt, both Joseph and Mary played decisive roles in the training and education of Jesus.

Little survives from antiquity concerning how Jewish parents approached the education of their children. Josephus wrote about the importance that parents attached to education and their legal responsibility to do so. Josephus wished to counter the accusations of some Greeks who were critical of many aspects of Jewish culture, including their religious and educational practices. In his work *Against Apion,* he stated:

> . . . it [the law] ordains that the very beginning of our education should be immediately directed to sobriety. It also commands us to bring those children up in learning, and to exercise them in the laws, and make them acquainted with the acts of their predecessors, in order to their imitation of them, and that they might be nourished up in the laws from their infancy, and might neither transgress them, nor have any pretence for their ignorance of them.[3]

Even before the formal training of a Jewish child began, he acquired some early instruction at home. He learned to speak his parents' language and to be obedient. Like his parents, Jesus spoke Aramaic and probably the dialect peculiar to Galilee. His dialect, however, cannot be firmly established as Galilean since both of his parents possessed ties to Judea, and Luke's account reveals that Mary had relatives still living in the hill country of Judea (1:39).[4]

A Jewish child was also taught to be obedient to authority in general (except when it conflicted with God's commandments) and to parents. Two of the first commandments given to a child were, "You shall have no other gods before me" (Ex. 20:3), and "Honor your father and your mother" (v. 12). Obedience was considered to be the foundation of all religious instruction, and disobedient children were considered to be spiritually foolish and rebellious (a major theme in the Book of Proverbs).

Once a child learned to speak and to be obedient, other training took place. Both parents of Jesus probably instructed Him in learning simple creeds of the Jewish faith and also in memorizing selected passages from the Torah. His first exposure to hymns probably consisted of the shorter psalms.

Following these tasks, the parents of Jesus continued their progressive education of their son. He was taught other passages of the Old Testament Scripture, short prayers, and bits and pieces of extrabiblical sayings of Jewish sages. Much of this was memorized so that a Jewish child was not ignorant of his faith in spite of his lack of literacy.

By age five or six, when hand and eye coordination had improved, actual reading and writing commenced. This undertaking could have occurred in either the home or in a synagogue school or both. Whether Nazareth's synagogue supported a school for youth instruction cannot be known, but certainly some instruction took place through the synagogue. A synagogue officer, the "hassan," had charge of this duty. Jesus probably received His first formative synagogue instruction during His middle childhood. That He was no stranger to the Nazareth synagogue during His years of upbringing was revealed in Luke 4:16: "And he came to Nazareth, where he had been brought up: and, as his custom was, he went into the synagogue on the sabbath day, and stood up for to read" (KJV).

This passage and John 8:6, where Jesus was recorded as writing, showed that Jesus could read and write. These skills were acquired during His childhood in Nazareth. Reading and writing not only were practical skills in first-century Galilee but were necessary to follow the Jewish faith since Jewish people had to familiarize themselves with the Old Testament and, in particular, the Torah.

The education of Christ almost certainly possessed a supernatural aspect. Perhaps this is what was implied by Luke 2:40: "The child grew and became strong, filled with wisdom; and the favor of God was upon him."

Observers of the young Jesus, however, would have seen nothing especially supernatural about His upbringing in this respect. Since the first-recorded miracle (or "sign") consisted of turning water into wine at Cana during a wedding feast (John 2:11), Jesus apparently chose not to exhibit His extraordinary abilities in any special way during this period of His life. To others He may have appeared to be bright, even a little precocious when He was a small boy, but there is no biblical or historical evidence that His hometown neighbors regarded Him in any way as a special or divinely gifted child.

In fact, to the contrary they often treated the adult Jesus with incredible disrespect in this regard. Their memories of Jesus during His upbringing in Nazareth did not include His being especially extraordinary, so they taunted Him. Once they asked each other, "Where did this man get this wisdom and these mighty works?" (Matt. 13:54; also see Mark 6:2).

Intertwined with His education, Jesus also learned the rituals of His faith. These included such observances as the dietary laws, the laws of separation, property regulations, and a host of other decrees of His faith. Judaism consisted of keeping the law and Jesus Himself diligently observed His faith and later in His adult life confirmed that He desired only to fulfill the law (Matt. 5:17-19).

The life of a Jewish child like Jesus was filled with religious obligations. This consisted of observing a weekly sabbath and a set of holidays, feasts, and fasts. In late winter or early spring, Purim, the Feast of Esther, broke the monotony of winter with celebrations and merriment. In spring Passover commemorated the delivery of the Israelites out of Egypt, while the Feast of Weeks signified the onset of summer. In autumn the New Year Feast, the fast of the Day of Atonement (Yom Kippur), and the Feast of Tabernacles were all observed in either celebration or in solemn reverence (Day of Atonement). The annual cycle of holidays (by our modern Christian way of reckoning) ended with the early winter celebration of Hanukkah, which commemorated the rededication of the temple by Judas Maccabee. From an early age Jesus, along with the household of His parents, kept these holidays that provided the background for many later events of His life (Luke 2:41; 22:1; John 7:2; 10:22; John 19:14, just to mention a few).

Temple Visit at Age Twelve

The Bible only records one incident from Jesus' childhood. The incident occurred in conjunction with a Jewish holiday— Jesus visited Jerusalem at age twelve for the Passover (Luke

2:41-50). This visit may have been taken place in any of the years between A.D. 4-8, depending on what year between 8-4 B.C. He was born (see chapter 3 for discussion of the chronology for the Nativity).

Ironically, the time of His visit to Jerusalem occurred during a highly eventful time in Jewish history. By A.D. 4 and 5 the subjects of Archelaus had become so weary of his rule that they protested loudly to Augustus. After hearing delegations of both the Jews and the Samaritans, the emperor removed Archelaus, banished him to Gaul (modern France), and instituted direct Roman rule of much of Palestine in A.D. 6. The governor of Syria, Quirinius, carried out a census and taxing that sparked a bloody revolt by Judas of Galilee.[5]

The revolt was eventually suppressed by A.D. 7, but tensions remained high for some time afterward. Depending on the year of the birth of Jesus, this temple visit fell either shortly before or after these events, and those events help explain Mary and Joseph's concern when they realized He was missing from their group that was returning from the feast (vv. 45,48).

The visit to the temple by the parents of Jesus had evidently been an annual event. This time, however, Jesus accompanied them. Luke's account does not reveal if this was Jesus' first visit, but the events that transpired showed that this visit was quite different from past visits for Joseph and Mary.

On the return trip from the Passover celebration, Joseph and Mary assumed that Jesus was among unnamed relatives and acquaintances. In fact, they went an entire day's journey from Jerusalem before inquiring about His whereabouts. When they questioned their relatives, Joseph and Mary discovered that Jesus was not with them. Because of the tensions generated by the fall or imminent fall of Archelaus and the threat or enactment of direct Roman rule with the possibility of violence, they became alarmed that Jesus was not among their traveling party. It was not a good time for a young boy to be missing.

In the meantime, Jesus was perfectly safe somewhere in the temple complex in Jerusalem. He had not even attempted to leave the city. For three days (while His parents went one day's journey, walked back, and found Him in the temple on the third day), he stayed among the rabbinical scholars, discussing their deepest religious concerns. Jesus both listened and asked questions of them. When the scholars questioned him, they were astonished at His understanding and the answers He gave. Their specific discussions were not recorded, but almost certainly they talked about the Passover observance and its meaning.

From the context of this passage, it seems clear that Jesus did not offend the assembled scholars during their discussions. They were impressed by what Jesus told them, and the fact that they would even discuss these deep religious topics with a mere boy underscores their astonishment at this very gifted young savant. Jesus stopped short of declaring Himself the ultimate Passover sacrifice or "the Lamb of God," but He provided the rabbis with a Passover they would not forget.

Arriving at the temple complex, the parents of Jesus found Him involved in one of these discussions. Bewildered by the developments of the past three days, they apparently were both relieved and upset at finding Jesus in the temple. It is not known in what area of the temple that Jesus conducted His discussions with the scholars. Probably the discussion took place in one of the outer areas to which women had access since the Luke account records Mary as speaking first to Jesus (v. 48).

Mary probably spoke to him in a voice both stern and sympathetic, "Son, why have you treated us so? Behold, your father and I have been looking for you anxiously."

Jesus gave what must have seemed to His parents a most peculiar answer: "How is it that you sought me? Did you not know that I must be in my Father's house?" (v. 49).

This statement signified that Jesus recognized His messianic mission. At what point previous to this incident He knew this cannot be known, but the biblical account has Him verbalizing the realization of His mission here. From this point forward Jesus prepared for His ministry.

This declaration also reveals that Jesus knew that Joseph was not His real father. Once again, how or when He came to know this cannot be ascertained since Mary preferred to keep silent on Jesus' origin after His birth (vv. 19,51), and Joseph had not possessed a reputation for discussing the events concerning His adopted son (Matt. 1:18-19). Besides, telling a young son that He was the Messiah was hardly something that parents could easily do. Mary's statement showed that even she desired to maintain the appearance that Joseph was the father of Jesus, even when both parents knew better (Luke 2:48).

This incident at the temple closed the chapter on the childhood of Jesus. A young boy who knew He was the Messiah could no longer be called a child. Eighteen years passed before Jesus' public ministry began, but already His Heavenly Father had begun the preparation for that ministry.

Jesus, however, still remained quite normal in many ways. After this incident of importance at the temple, Luke records that He returned to Nazareth with His parents, obeying the commandment to "Honor your father and your mother" and obeying His parents (v. 51).

8

The "Silent Years": Thirteen to Thirty

And he went down with them, and came to Nazareth, and was obedient to them; and his mother kept all these things in her heart. And Jesus increased in wisdom and in stature, and in favor with God and man (Luke 2:51-52).

The period of Jesus's life from age thirteen to thirty has commonly been referred to as the silent years. This period acquired this title because the record of His life contained in the four Gospels does not mention a single incident during this time of His life. The Gospel accounts, nevertheless, have revealed glimpses of this time "between the lines" of the recorded events of His later public ministry. In fact, the silent years actually speak quite loudly in some areas of His life, such as His family life, occupation, continuing education, and preparation for His later public ministry.

Another look at the history of Palestine after the fall of Archelaus and the institution of direct Roman rule of Judea to the beginning of His public ministry could be helpful in understanding this part of the life of Christ. With public order restored by Roman troops and Herodian mercenaries, anti-Roman insurrections died down after A.D. 7. Even the death of Augustus in A.D. 14 and the ascension of the relatively anti-Jewish Emperor Tiberius did not lead to any major Jewish upheavals on the scale seen in 4 B.C. and A.D. 6-7.

The ascension of Tiberius, nevertheless, incurred the displeasure of the Jews both in and out of Palestine. Tiberius reigned A.D. 14-37 and hardly proved to be a friend of the Jews. He continued his adopted father's policy of direct Roman rule and taxation of Judea and sent a number of Roman governors to enforce these unpopular measures. His later decision to send Pontius Pilate, the least sensitive governor of

Judea, to rule that area led to the greatest unrest in Judea since A.D. 6-7. In the capital city of Rome, Tiberius eventually decided to ban Judaism and banished over four thousand Jews to Sardinia while sending uncounted others into military service. In spite of these measures, however, Tiberius refrained from goading Palestinian Jews into outright revolt, although many Jews of this period desired an end of direct Roman rule.[1]

The high priests of this period cooperated with the Roman authorities, and the family of Annas—composed of himself, his sons, and his son-in-law Joseph Caiaphas—dominated the office of the high priest throughout much of the reign of Tiberius. These aristocratic Sadducees opposed the nationalistic tendencies of the anti-Roman Zealots and later of Jesus and His followers. Their fear of a Roman overreaction to Zealot activity led them to demand the death of Jesus ("it was expedient that one man should die for the people"—John 18:14).[2]

Roman rule of Judea and the spinelessness of the Jewish aristocracy promoted further messianic expectation throughout the period before the public ministry of Jesus. The hated Roman policy of direct taxation bore heavily on the Jewish conscience and the tax collector or publican found in the four Gospels became linked in the popular mind as being "the chief of sinners," and even was tied to other groups of despised sinners, such as prostitutes and thieves. Roman rule and misrule of Judea was a continual source of irritation among the Jews.

The Herodian rulers of the northern and Transjordan areas of Palestine, who professed Judaism, fared a little better in the eyes of many of their subjects. The Herods, however, were little more than "Roman rule by proxy." Philip II, who governed districts of northeast Palestine, largely ruled over non-Jewish subjects. Strongly attracted to Greco-Roman culture, he rebuilt the city of Panias at the headwaters of the Jordan and named it Caesarea Philippi, "the Caesarea of Philip" to distinguish it from his father's Caesarea on the Mediterranean coast, built in honor of the family of the emperor. He also rebuilt the town of Bethsaida, renaming it Julias in honor of the daughter of Augustus. In spite of Philip's identification with both his Gentile subjects and culture, however, neither the New Testament authors nor ancient Jewish sources wrote anything negative about him. Josephus even praised him as "a person of moderation and quietness." Nevertheless, the Jews of his tetrarchy knew where he stood on the issue of Roman rule either dirctly or indirectly.[3]

Herod Antipas, the tetrarch of Galilee and Transjordan Perea, however, continued to be a poor ruler during the period after A.D. 6-7. He was a merciless tyrant who was dominated by his ambitious wife, Herodias. He kept tabs on Galilean Zealot activity and pursued a slavish loyalty to Emperor Tiberius and a strong attachment to Greco-Roman culture that upset his Jewish subjects. He honored his friendship with the emperor by building a city named Tiberias on the shores of the Sea of Galilee. This, however, further offended Jewish Galileans. When only Gentiles responded to settling the city, Antipas compelled Jewish Galileans to live there in spite of their protests that he had demolished a cemetery to make room for the city and had not observed the proper purification rituals (Num. 19:11-13). Antipas, hated by many of his Jewish subjects, was destined to have a part in the deaths of two of his most famous subjects—John the Baptist and Jesus.[4]

In such an environment, Jesus grew to manhood. He observed firsthand the messianic expectations of His people, as well as the corruption spawned by Roman and Herodian rule. The Galilee of Herodians and Zealots, Jews and Gentiles, and sinners and saints became the homeland of the developing young Messiah.

The Home Life of Jesus of Nazareth

From age thirteen until the beginning of His public ministry, Jesus lived at Nazareth in the home of His parents. Luke's account records that Jesus was subject to His parents (2:51). In spite of Jesus' awakening preparation for His coming mission, He continued to keep the Fifth Commandment to "honor your father and your mother." Even the Messiah had to obey His parents, and Jesus apparently remained under the authority of both parents, and later just the surviving parent, for roughly eighteen years after His visit to the temple.

While Jesus obeyed His parents in part as an obligation of the law, He also genuinely loved them. Little reliable information exists about the commitment of Jesus to His parents during the years of His upbringing in Nazareth; nevertheless, it can be assumed that they enjoyed a warm and loving relationship. Perhaps desiring the company of His parents, Jesus may have escorted his mother on her water trips to "Mary's Well" and helped Joseph in the carpenter shop. Joseph's home in Nazareth provided a loving environment for Jesus, whose religious movement was based on love. Actually the household in which Jesus grew up contained a rather large family: two parents, Jesus, brothers named James, Joseph (or Joses), Judas (or Jude), and Simon, and at least two unnamed sisters (Matt. 13:55-56; Mark 6:3). (See Figure 7 for Jesus' family.)

More than likely, these brothers and sisters of Jesus were also the offspring of both Joseph and Mary. In spite of the assertion of Roman Catholic and Greek Orthodox theologians that these siblings were the children of Joseph by a previous marriage and therefore not related to Jesus by blood, biblical evidence seems to favor their parentage by both Joseph and Mary. After all, Mary did not remain a perpetual virgin after the birth of Jesus (Matt. 1:25), and none of the Gospel accounts have specifically stated that these brothers and sisters of Jesus belonged to Joseph by a previous marriage.

A further indication that Jesus was a sibling of these children by both Joseph and Mary is the assertion of two of the Gospels that Jesus was the "firstborn." This could imply that Mary gave birth to other children. Admittedly, there is much room for dispute on this point. The Old Testament use of the term "firstborn" in the law of Moses does not necessarily imply that other children follow. Also, the older Greek, Latin,

Figure 7
Known Biblical Family Members and Relatives of Jesus

Family Member or Relative	Relationship to Jesus
Joseph	Earthly Father
Mary	Mother
James	Brother
Joseph (or Joses)	Brother
Judas (or Jude)	Brother
Simon	Brother
Sister I[a]	Sister
Sister II[a]	Sister
Mary[b]	Aunt
Elizabeth	Cousin
John the Baptist	Cousin

_____

[a]"Sisters mentioned in Matthew 13:56 and Mark 6:3, but their number and names are not recorded in the Bible. Early tradition said there were two—Assia and Lydia. This tradition was preserved in the apocryphal *The History of Joseph the Carpenter,* 2.

[b]John 19:25. Some believe this aunt could be the woman Salome mentioned in Mark 15:40.

and Aramaic manuscripts of Matthew 1:25 left out the term "firstborn" (KJV).

Nevertheless, the Gospels do not record that Mary specifically remained childless after the birth of Jesus. Also, even the oldest manuscripts of Luke 2:7 contain the term "firstborn" (KJV) and even if a later well-meaning copyist lifted the phrase from Luke to Matthew, the validity of the firstborn status of Jesus cannot be substantially altered.

Moreover, other passages in the Gospels relating to Jesus' public ministry mention Mary and the siblings of Jesus as a family unit (Matt. 12:46-50; 13:55-58; Mark 6:3; Acts 1:14). If these siblings were all other half-brothers and sisters from a previous marriage of Joseph, they would have been on their own by the time of the public ministry of Jesus and not remaining together with their step-mother. In fact, some of them could have been young at the time of Jesus' crucifixion and that may explain why Jesus appointed the "beloved disciple" to look after His mother (John 19:25-27).

The relationship between Jesus and these younger brothers appeared to be strained by the time of Jesus' later public ministry, and the causes for this probably developed in their formative years in Nazareth. Joseph and Mary unintentionally may have favored Jesus over His brothers during this time. The brothers, in turn, may have grown resentful of Him. Later this strained relationship revealed itself in two incidents during the public ministry of Jesus: when Jesus apparently refused to see His impatient family (Matt. 12:46-50) and when His brothers disbelieved in Him at the time of the Feast of Tabernacles (John 7:1-9).

Fortunately for the family of Jesus, the disarray of relations between the brothers ended at the report of the resurrection. His brothers were numbered among the apostles after the ascension of Jesus (Acts 1:13-14). His brother James later headed the Jerusalem church until his martyrdom, and the office of bishop of Jerusalem remained in the Lord's family until the time of Emperor Trajan (A.D. 98-117). James and Jude each wrote a general (or catholic) epistle, and Symeon, a cousin of the Lord named as bishop of Jerusalem after James, died a martyr's death at age 120. That such faith did not exist during the year of Jesus' upbringing and public ministry was viewed by later Christians as a fulfillment of a verse in a messianic psalm, "I have become a stranger to my brethren and an alien to my mothers' sons" (Ps. 69:8).[5]

The relationship between Jesus and His sisters cannot be determined from any reliable source. We know neither how many sisters He had nor their names. Early tradition, however, said there were two, and they were named Assia and Lydia, although in some manuscripts Assia is called Anna. The earliest written account on the sisters of Jesus dates from the fourth century in the apocryphal *The History of Joseph the Carpenter.* This work, unreliable and often in conflict with information in the Gospels, has little validity in recalling any legitimate tradition about the upbringing of Jesus. Nevertheless, it contains the earliest information we possess on the number and names of the sisters of Jesus (see note *a* of Figure 7).

As the growing family of Joseph and Mary sank roots into the community of Nazareth, the family underwent many changes. Jesus helped His father in the carpentry trade as He reached His teenage years, while His younger siblings remained under Mary's guidance. This arrangement changed as the siblings grew older. The younger boys also assisted their father and Jesus assumed the role of Joseph's apprentice.

This decision soon proved to be a wise one, for Joseph died sometime between the temple visit when Jesus was twelve and the beginning of His public ministry. That Joseph died during this period can be proved by His omission in the Gospel record of the public ministry of Jesus, even though His mother, brothers, and sisters were mentioned. Though we possess no reliable record of how old Jesus was when Joseph died, He was probably old enough to carry on the family business.

From Joseph's death until Jesus' public ministry began, the large family was held together by Jesus. In addition to being the breadwinner, He officiated at family religious functions and acted as de facto father to His younger siblings. He may have asked some of His brothers to assist Him in His carpentry business, although no reliable tradition said they followed Him in this trade, and third- and fourth-century tradition said that His brothers James and Jude became farmers for a while in their adult years.

When Jesus finally left His family to pursue His public

ministry, His family must have been concerned. After all, He was ultimately responsible for their financial well-being. Their concerns about income and the fate of the family business would have been very great. Nevertheless, He must have reminded them that His ministry had to take precedence even over His family obligations. He may have been reflecting on this experience when He told the apostles, "A man's foes will be those of his own household. He who loves father or mother more than me is not worthy of me; and he who loves son or daughter more than me is not worthy of me; and he who does not take up his cross and follow after me is not worthy of me" (Matt. 10:36-38). By age thirty or so (Luke 3:23), Jesus was ready to begin.

Other Relatives and Acquaintances of Jesus

Jesus had kinship ties with an extended family (see Fig. 7). Some are mentioned by name in biblical accounts. Though Elizabeth and her son, John the Baptist, were Jesus' cousins (relatives), scholars of the New Testament have found no evidence to show that the cousins ever met before Jesus was baptized by John. One verse in Luke reports that unnamed relatives accompanied Joseph and Mary on the return to Nazareth when Jesus stayed with the scholars in Jerusalem (2:44). An aunt of Jesus later stood by the cross, but other relatives in His extended family were largely ignored by the Gospel writers (John 19:25).

Jesus certainly possessed friends and acquaintances during His years of upbringing in Nazareth. Tradition and the largely unreliable "infancy narratives" of later centuries provided Jesus with many named playmates and peers during His stay in Nazareth, but these friends have not been mentioned by even fairly reliable church fathers. Other tradition has assigned some of the apostles as boyhood friends of Jesus. Reasonable speculation suggests that some of the apostles might have at least known Jesus before His public ministry, but, again, no direct biblical evidence or reliable tradition supports this speculation.

Occupation of Jesus

During the years before His public ministry, Jesus earned a living for His family as a carpenter (Mark 6:3). Other than this reference in Mark and one in Matthew (13:55), few other reliable sources on His carpentry trade have survived. Justin Martyr, a second-century Palestinian from Samaria, probably recorded a local Galilean tradition concerning the Lord's preministry occupation. He wrote:

> He was considered to be the son of Joseph the carpenter, and he appeared without comeliness as the Scriptures declared, and he was deemed a carpenter. For he was in the habit of working as a carpenter when among men, making ploughs and yokes, by which He taught the symbols of righteousness and an active life.[6]

Jesus chose an occupation that was relatively new among Palestinian Jews. In the Old Testament the carpentry/woodworking trade in Israel tended to be dominated by foreigners (usually Phoenicians from Tyre and Sidon). When David built his palace in Jerusalem, he imported Phoenician carpenters (2 Sam. 5:11; 1 Chron. 14:1); when Solomon constructed the temple, he resorted to the same source (1 Kings 5:6). A few centuries later, Zerubbabel still had to depend on Phoenician woodcutters and carpenters to rebuild the temple (Ezra 3:7).

Carpentry in the ancient world was far less specialized than it is today. In antiquity the line between woodworking and carpentry hardly existed. Carpenters who made household furniture and farming tools during one week would build small boats and work on houses the next week. Since most Jewish houses in the early New Testament era were largely constructed of stone, few carpenters engaged in full-time home building. Compared to today's carpenter, ancient carpenters were far more versatile.

Carpentry, then and now, tended to be a type of work that demanded physical exertion and mental skill. This occupation caused a man to work very hard for long days, often outdoors, exposed to sun and wind. This vocation molded Jesus into a strong man. This active life later enabled Him to bear some of the harsh physical demands of His ministry, such as standing while delivering lengthy sermons to thousands of people, staying up all night to pray, walking throughout much of Palestine, fasting for forty days, and enduring the torture and mistreatment of His passion.

In addition to the physical demands of carpentry, it also required mental skill. A carpenter had to calculate, measure, cut, and assemble desired piecework in methodical fashion. Good carpenters could routinely measure lengths of wood without resorting to measuring instruments. While many nonprofessional carpenters claim to have picked up their abilities rather quickly, an experienced professional carpenter acquired his skills as a result of years of on-the-job training.

Interestingly enough, carpentry required a number of attributes that Jesus later found useful in His public ministry, such as patience, planning as a prerequisite to an undertaking, carrying out the request of others and filling their orders to their specifications, taking raw materials and molding them into a finished product, and persuading His followers to trust in His workmanship. Jesus, the maker of yokes, after all, later told His disciples, "Take my yoke upon you and learn from me; for I am gentle and lowly in heart, and you will find rest for your souls. For my yoke is easy and my burden is light" (Matt. 11:29-30).

Continuing Education of Jesus

When Jesus began His carpentry vocation, His formal education largely came to an end. His education, however, continued in more informal ways. As revealed in Luke 4:16, Jesus was in the habit of standing up to read in the synagogue on the sabbath day. His knowledge of the Law and Prophets probably owed much to the sabbath-day instruction He had received from childhood.

Since Jesus later quoted from nearly every Old Testament

book, He must have studied the Law and the Prophets on His own. Perhaps the Nazareth synagogue or wealthy neighbors possessed a complete or nearly complete set of Old Testament books. Gaining access to these books was a relatively easy task for a faithful student, and Jesus fulfilled that qualification. Since the later Gospel writers usually favored quoting from the Greek Septuagint version of the Old Testament, reasonable speculation suggests that Jesus may have been familiar with that version as well.[7]

Jesus' knowledge of Greek and Latin was extensive and, as events in His public ministry proved, He conversed with those who spoke those languages as their first tongue. The Greek woman of Phoenicia, the Roman centurion, and Pilate (Mark 7:26; Matt. 8:13; and John 18:33-34) conversed with Jesus, and these dialogues could have been in Greek or Latin. Jesus could have learned these languages in multicultural Galilee during His years of upbringing in Nazareth.

As the time for His public ministry neared, Jesus reached the zenith of the fruits of His education. From the time Jesus discussed religion with the Jewish religious leaders in the Temple at age twelve, His knowledge of Jewish Scripture and tradition associated with it had been growing. He also had learned to read and write, had become an astute observer of Gentile culture, and was either familiar with or knew Greek and Latin. With His education fulfilled, He made plans to leave His home in Nazareth.

The Physical Appearance of Jesus

The physical appearance of Jesus can never be known. He began His ministry in His early thirties. However, a reference in the Gospel of John suggests that He may have looked a little older than His age. His enemies said of Him. "You are not yet fifty years old, and have you seen Abraham?" (John 8:57) Apparently they thought He was in His forties. If He gave the appearance of being in His thirties during that time of His life, they would have asked, "You are not yet forty years old, and have you seen Abraham?"

The postapostolic age (after A.D. 100) created artistic representations of Jesus. Unfortunately for us today, these portrayals assure us that they too were guessing. Literary speculation on Jesus' appearance tends to be just as unreliable. Early postapostolic art shows Jesus as a young beardless youth or a middle-aged bearded man. Eusebius, the early-fourth-century church historian, mentioned a Palestinian statue of Jesus that supposedly dated from the first century, but Jewish-Christians of that era would not have erected a statue of Jesus for fear of running afoul of the Old Testament ban on making images (Ex. 20:4).[8]

Therefore, our only reliable clues to Jesus' appearance must come from the Scriptures, and few are supplied. While traditions of His appearance either portray Him as exceptionally handsome or incredibly plain, it is obvious from a few scriptural incidents that He looked rather ordinary. All four Gospels mention that on the night of His arrest, Judas Iscariot was needed to single out Jesus from the eleven apostles. If Jesus were reputed to be either extremely handsome or ugly, Judas would not have employed his prearranged identification kiss. At no point either before or during His public ministry are we told that He appeared to look exceptional in any way. While all four Gospel report the often vicious remarks of His enemies, none included a direct reference to taunts about His appearance. Since such references are lacking, we possibly can conclude that Jesus presented an average appearance to those who saw Him.

He probably wore clothes similar to that of other men of His day. He dressed in the two standard garments—a tunic and a cloak. Both were made from either wool or linen. The tunic, often mistranslated in some Bible versions as *coat*, was actually worn as an undergarment that would look like a long shirt. The cloak, or outer garment, was worn over the tunic and doubled as an overcoat by day and as a blanket by night. For footwear, He wore sandals. Sandals usually were made with a sole of wood or leather that was fastened to the foot by leather straps. Few men of this era possessed shoes that covered the whole foot. Since sandals left feet exposed to the dust of Palestinian roads, the hospitality custom of footwashing after a day's travel developed. During His public ministry, Jesus wore all of these items of apparel (Matt. 3:11; Mark 1:7; Luke 3:16; John 19:23-24).

More than likely, He also wore a wide belt (called a *girdle* in some translations) and a headdress. If a tunic was ungirded, men strapped on a wide belt. This allowed them to walk about more freely and also to use the belt as a means of attaching tools or other items to their persons. The belt was usually made from leather or cloth. John the Baptist possessed a leather belt (Matt. 3:4); Jesus may have owned one, too, but the Scriptures do not give us such details. Jesus also may have donned a headdress of some type. While widely used by Jewish men of this era, the Gospels do not mention Jesus' wearing one. This headdress, either a turban (Job. 29:14; Isa. 3:23) or a head veil much like the modern *kaffieh* favored by Arab herdsmen, provided protection from the hot Palestinian sun.

Since the law of Moses commanded Jews not to disfigure their beards or to shave the corners of their heads, Jesus wore a beard and may have allowed the corner locks of His hair to grow out (Lev. 19:27). In the Old Testament era, many Jewish men valued long hair, and no prohibition against it is recorded (2 Sam. 14:26; Song of Sol. 5:11). In the surviving art of antiquity, captive Jews are portrayed with long hair. Jesus, too, probably followed this fashion in contrast to the Roman rulers of much of Palestine who were clean-shaven and short-haired. Ironically, the apostle Paul later endorsed the Roman short-haired fashion for the largely Romanized Corinthian church (1 Cor. 11:14).

Like most Jews of the first century, Jesus wore a beard. The beard was usually uncut and, therefore, grew rather long. On the eve of His public ministry, Jesus' beard and hair may have been streaked with gray since some thought He looked older than His age. He may have followed the fashion of His day in oiling and perfuming His hair and beard, but this action is not mentioned in the Gospels, though Jesus once alluded to the custom (Luke 7:46).

Besides these few comments, the Gospels writers did not record much on the appearance of Jesus. Descriptions of how He looked were not central to their concerns about His ministry and teachings. Nevertheless, what little is known about His appearance has in part both confirmed and dismissed aspects of His traditional portrayal in the arts.

The End of His Private Life in Nazareth

Nearing the age of thirty or perhaps a little past that age, Jesus knew that His public ministry was at hand. Old Testament Scripture specified that a life of religious service for the Levites and priests could begin only after the age of thirty (Num. 4:3,23,47). Although many Old Testament prophets and kings first held offices in these capacities at various ages, thirty became a traditional age for these offices as well. Saul began his reign as king at age thirty, as did the ancestor of Jesus—King David (2 Sam. 5:4). Jesus too fulfilled the traditional age for formal service in the Lord's work as an archetype prophet, priest, and king (Luke 3:23).

To pinpoint chronologically the year Jesus began His public ministry is difficult in spite of information in Luke (vv. 1-23). Luke's chronological clues in verses 1-3 were given to date the beginning of John the Baptist's ministry, not that of the Lord's ministry. John, six months older than Jesus, began his ministry at least six months before that of his more famous relative. This ministry could have lasted longer than six months because Jesus was baptized at an undetermined time during John's ministry, shortly before undertaking His own public ministry.

The clues in Luke 3:1-3, nevertheless, point to a rough estimate of the beginnings of both John's ministry and also that of Jesus. The "fifteenth year of the reign of Tiberius Caesar" dates the genesis of John's ministry sometime in the year A.D. 28/29 since Tiberius began his reign in A.D. 14. Therefore, Jesus must have started His ministry sometime around A.D. 29-30.[9]

Jesus, hearing of John's ministry, made preparations for His own mission. He knew John was His forerunner—"the one crying in the wilderness of Judea" (see Isa. 40:3). Having realized that His days in Nazareth were numbered, He made plans to ensure His mother's family was provided for in His absence.

These preparations for the provision of His household cannot be known to us today, but they certainly took place. Jesus, along with His mother, knew that this time would occur. Perhaps savings had been accumulated by that time, or one or more of His half-brothers were old enough to support the family. Both of these options may have transpired. Whatever happened, Jesus left only after He had provided for the needs of His family.

In fact, we possess no record of any material need being neglected in regard to Jesus' family during His public ministry. On many occasions, His family either accompanied Him or met Him in the course of His travels. They, however, did not ask Jesus for any funds or provisions for themselves in the Gospel records. Only at the cross when Jesus asked the "beloved disciple" to take care of His mother do we have any faint record of a family member of Jesus needing any special attention during His public ministry (see John 19:25-27).

When these preparations were taken care of, Jesus began a spiritual preparation for His undertaking. This must have consisted of a period of prayer and meditation. He may have fasted, although a fast too close to His baptism seems unlikely since Jesus endured a forty-day fast after His baptism (Matt. 4:1-2; Mark 1:12-13; Luke 4:1-2). Jesus awaited only the call of the Spirit to begin His journey to be baptized by John.

Meanwhile, John had started his ministry as the forerunner for the Messiah. He preached and baptized at at least three locales on the Jordan River: the wilderness of Judea at the mouth of the Jordan (Matt. 3:1); Bethabara (or Bethany in some manuscripts) in Transjordan Perea—perhaps the actual place of Jesus' baptism (John 1:28); and Aenon near Salim, much upstream from the river's mouth (John 3:23). Luke, however, points out that John's ministry took place at other unnamed locations throughout the Jordan Valley (3:3).

John's mission was to prepare the Jewish people for the Messiah, urging them to repent of their sins and submit to baptism by his hand in the Jordan River. John urged all the Jews to repent, including the tax collectors, the wealthy, and the Herodian (Jewish) soldiers. Even the religious leaders did not escape his sharp rebuke, and he compared them to snakes (Matt. 3:7).

Among the common people, however, John acquired a large following and remained popular in spite of his rough appearance and bizarre diet of locusts and wild honey (Matt. 3:4). John's reputation for austere righteousness later prompted Jesus to call him "the greatest man ever born of a woman" (see 11:11), made Herod Antipas to fear him because of his popularity among the people, and even caused the religious leaders to recognize the fact that the multitudes regarded him as a prophet (Matt. 14:5; 21:26).

John's call to the prophetic ministry aroused the religious authorities. They regarded the prophetic call as their own possession and resented his intrusion into their spiritual territory. They also noticed that John apparently had neglected the traditional function expected of him in the law. Although he was a Levite and the son of a priest (Luke 1:5), he took up no duties in the priesthood or the Levitical order in Jerusalem. Instead he went to the wilderness of Judea and started his own ministry. To our knowledge, John never conducted a ministry in Jerusalem or in the temple. Therefore, the religious leaders found it easy to reject John's calling (Matt. 21:25).

A summary of John's ministry can be gleaned from the pages of the four Gospels. He preached that the Messiah's days was imminent and urged all Jews to submit to his baptism of repentance for the remission of sins. Some of his teachings must have seemed radically harsh at times. He rebuked the religious leaders, urged listeners to give away their spare clothes and extra food to those who had none, told tax collectors to take only the money appointed to them (therefore receiving no profit), ordered soldiers not to intimidate anyone and to be content with their pay, and denounced Herod Antipas the Tetrarch for marrying his brother's wife. John's appearance and diet also betrayed a bent toward asceticism and perhaps a Nazarite vow (Num. 6:1-21). In spite of this, however, he became all the more popular among the people who continued to flock to him.

While John may have been popular, he tended to be a humble man who discounted his importance. He dressed roughly and ate simply. While Jesus later spoke of him as a spiritual manifestation of Elijah (Matt. 17:10-13), John himself denied that he was a literal reincarnation of that prophet (John 1:21). This downplaying of his importance endeared him to his more famous relative who later told His own disciples, "for everyone who exalts himself will be humbled, and he who humbles himself will be exalted" (Luke 18:14).

Before Jesus went to John for baptism, the two relatives had apparently never met face to face (John 1:31,33), or at least not in the roles of forerunner and Messiah. John knew he was the forerunner; he did not know his own cousin was the Messiah. For His part, Jesus knew John as the forerunner from both the probable testimony of His mother and revelation from the Spirit. As John's ministry progressed, Jesus awaited the day He would travel to John for His baptism.

On some day unknown to us, that time arrived. Jesus left Nazareth and journeyed to the place on the Jordan where John was preaching. Jesus' carpentry trade, home life, and years of preparation for public ministry had come to an end. Jesus the Carpenter and Jesus the Nazarene were now replaced by Jesus Christ—the Messiah.[10]

While making the journey, Jesus surely must have pondered over the abrupt changes about to take place in His life.

The private security of Nazareth was to be superseded by His upcoming baptism, public ministry, passion, and resurrection. The events facing Him must have excited and troubled Him, but He was resolved to accomplish them with a divine determination.

Conclusion

With the journey to the Jordan River for baptism at the hands of John, the chapters of Jesus' life before His public ministry were closed. Jesus the Messiah had been molded by the events and experiences of the previous thirty or so years. Bethlehem, Egypt, Jerusalem, and Nazareth each left their mark on His development as He would one day leave His mark on them. His life and preparations in each locale had a strong bearing on His ministry and mission.

His life after his baptism tends to be covered much better by the Gospel writers than the events of His life prior to His public ministry. Even non-Christian writers of antiquity like Tacitus, Suetonius, and Josephus wrote small passages or allusions to His public ministry.

Before giving a brief epilogue of the remaining years of the Lord on this earth, it might be helpful to mention the earthly destiny of the many people who crossed His life during the first thirty or so years. Some like His earthly father Joseph, His brothers James and Judas, Herod the Great, Archelaus, and the Emperor Augustus have already been discussed in this account. Nothing relatively reliable has survived, however, concerning the later events of the lives of Zacharias, Elizabeth, the shepherds of Bethlehem, Simeon, Anna, the Magi, and most of His brothers and sisters.

Of others, we do possess some information derived from the

New Testament and other sources from antiquity. Mary, the mother of Jesus, witnessed the death of her son on the cross (John 19:25-27), continued to fellowship with the disciples after the ascension of Jesus (Acts 1:14), and, according to early tradition, spent some of her remaining earthly years in the home of John, the beloved disciple.

John the Baptist baptized Jesus and continued his own ministry until he was arrested by Herod Antipas. Herodias, the wife of Antipas, conspired with her daughter, Salome, to put John to death and tricked Antipas into ordering John's execution (Matt. 14:1-2; Mark 6:14-29; and Luke 9:7-9). According to Josephus (*Antiquities,* 18,5,2), John was put to death in Herod's fort at Macherus.

Quirinius (Cyrenius) lived for some time after his numerous Eastern assignments under Emperor Augustus—in fact, well into the reign of Tiberius. Late in life, Quirinius had acquired the reputation of being mean and cruel to those around him. He accused his divorced wife, Lepida, of adultery and attempting to poison him. Tiberius and the senate eventually supported Quirinius in the charge of attempted murder and banished her, although many prominent citizens sympathized with her. Not long after his ex-wife's trial, Quirinius died, and Tiberius requested that the senate vote him a public funeral. The people, however, remembered his mistreatment of Lepida and had little heart for honoring the old soldier and diplomat.[1]

Herod Antipas, the malevolent ruler of Galilee and Perea, continued to misrule his subjects. Besides executing John the Baptist, he later mocked Jesus during His interrogation in Jerusalem. When Jesus kept silent and refused to acknowledge Herod's request for a miracle, Herod and his soldiers clothed him in a royal robe and sent Jesus back to Pilate (Luke 23:7-12).

A few years later, Herodias inflamed her husband, Antipas, with the accusation that Herod Agrippa I was about to be appointed king of the tetrarchy previously held by Herod Philip II. She then demanded that Antipas also ask Emperor

Gaius (Caligula) for the title of king as well. Shortly afterward, they discovered that Herod Agrippa I would eventually acquire that title, and Antipas sailed for Rome to get an audience with the emperor. Agrippa's agent, however, convinced the emperor that Antipas was planning to conspire with the Parthians against the Romans and cited the dubious but potentially damaging proof that Antipas had maintained enough armor to arm seventy thousand men. Ironically, the tetrarch was innocent of the charge of conspiring with the Parthians, but he admitted that he possessed that much armor. The emperor stripped Antipas of his tetrarchy, assigned it to Agrippa, and banished both Herod Antipas and Herodias to Lyon in Gaul (France). The greed of the couple caused their own exile in A.D. 39 and removed the aging and corrupt Antipas from the office he had for forty-three years—years that coincided with most of the earthly years of Jesus.[2]

Tiberius was the Roman emperor during the teenage and adult years of Jesus who appointed Pontius Pilate as governor of Judea. Tiberius lived for only a few years after the passion week that encompassed the trial, death, and resurrection of Christ. Suspicious and brooding, Tiberius either imprisoned or executed many members of Rome's imperial family for fear they would be potential rivals. He was encouraged in this by his adviser Sejanus. Eventually, Sejanus plotted to depose the emperor, but Tiberius got wind of it and put him and his closest followers to death. On March 16, A.D. 37, Tiberius died on a trip to the island of Capri. While some people were suspicious that he had been slowly poisoned by his successor Gaius Caligula, Tacitus in his *Annals* recorded that Tiberius was actually smothered to death by the guard commander Macro with the encouragement of Caligula.[3]

As for Jesus, He submitted to John's baptism and embarked on an earthly ministry for over three years. During that time He taught His disciples a new faith that differed radically from traditional Judaism. Eventually He fulfilled His mission to die for mankind at Calvary outside Jerusalem. On the third day, He rose from the dead. According to the New

Testament records that He gave His disciples further instruction for forty days and then ascended back to heaven. Before He ascended, He commanded His followers to proclaim His message to others all over the world. Today nearly one billion people claim the label of *Christian*—a follower of Christ.

Appendix 1
Matthew's Genealogy of Jesus[a]

Abraham to David:[b]
Abraham—Isaac—Jacob—Judah—Perez (by Tamar)—Hezron—Ram—Amminadab—Nahshon—Salmon—Boaz (by Rahab)—Obed (by Ruth)—Jesse—David the king.

David to the Babylonian Captivity:
David — Solomon (by Bathsheba, the former wife of Uriah Hittite)—Rehoboam—Abijah—Asa—Jehoshaphat—Joram—Uzziah—Jotham—Ahaz—Hezekiah—Manasseh—Amos—Josiah—Jeconiah.

The Captivity of Jesus:
Jeconiah—Shealtiel—Zerubbabel—Abiud—Eliakim—Azor—Zadok—Achim—Eliud—Eleazar—Matthan—Jacob—Joseph (the husband of Mary, of whom Jesus was born).

---

[a]This genealogy represents the legal ancestry of Jesus through His earthly father, Joseph. Nevertheless, the Matthew account plainly reveals that only Mary was related to Jesus by blood. This account derives from Matthew 1:1-17.

[b]Obviously Matthew chose to give an abridged account of the Lord's ancestry. A few generations are skipped in this list. For a complete genealogy of the Lord see 1 Chronicles 1–4.

Appendix 2
Luke's Genealogy of Jesus[a]

Adam to Abraham:[b]
Adam—Seth—Enos—Cainan—Mahalaleel—Jared—Enoch—Methuselah—Lamech—Noah—Shem—Arphaxad—Cainan—Shelah—Eber—Peleg—Reu—Serug—Nahor—Terah—Abraham.

Abraham to David:
Abraham—Isaac—Jacob—Judah—Perez—Hezron—Arni—Admin—Amminadab—Nahshon—Sala—Boaz—Obed—Jesse—David.

David to Jesus:
David—Nathan—Mattatha—Menna—Melea—Eliakim—Jonam—Joseph—Judah—Simeon—Levi—Matthat—Jorim—Eliezer—Joshua—Er—Elmadam—Cosam—Addi—Melchi—Neri—Shealtiel—Zerubbabel—Rhesa—Joannan—Joda—Josech—Semein—Mattathias—Maath-Naggai—Esli—Nahum—Amos—Mattathias—Joseph—Jannai—Melchi—Levi—Matthat—Heli—Joseph—Jesus (supposed to be the son of Joseph).

---

[a]Luke 3:23-38. This account of Jesus' ancestry is given in the reverse order.

[b]For an explanation of the two variant genealogies see note 3 of Chapter 1.

Notes

CHAPTER 1

1. For the first five centuries of the Christian era, Christians fiercely debated the biblically based beliefs of the preincarnate existence of Christ, as well as the degree of His earthly divinity and humanity. Groups later labeled as heretical, such as the Jewish-Christian sects, Gnostics, Monophysites, and Monothelites, objected to one or both of these doctrines. From 325 to 500, numerous ecumenical councils were called to define these and other Christological issues (Trinity, etc.). By the year 500 the preincarnate existence of Christ along with the coequality of His two earthly natures (divine and human) won out as the more orthodox position among most practicing Christians.

2. Some writers of the life of Christ, notably Alfred Edersheim in his work *The Life and Times of Jesus the Messiah* (New York, 1923), believed that the "course of Abijah" may help date the annunciation to Zacharias and, therefore, also pinpoint the birth of Christ. This speculation, however, cannot be precisely proved as Edersheim later explained. Luke's reference to a course of the priesthood was designed to show the legitimacy of Zacharias's ministry and should not be interpreted as a time reference. The year, month, and day of the annunciation to Zacharias and the birth of Jesus cannot be determined with any reliable precision.

3. No serious attempt at reconciling the two genealogies found in Matthew 1:1-17 and Luke 3:23-38 can ever be successful. They are obviously two different genealogies. One interpretation, dating back to Annius of Viterbo in 1502, may be that the one in Matthew belongs to Joseph and represents Jesus' legal ancestry through His earthly father Joseph. Luke's genealogy belongs to Mary and represents the actual human ancestry of Jesus through His mother. This popular interpretation places Heli as Joseph's father-in-law rather than his father (Luke 3:23). A further indication of this is the observation that the events of Matthew 1—2 seemingly derive indirectly from Joseph, while the events of Luke 1—2, and perhaps the genealogy in 3 ultimately originate with Mary.

On the other hand, the early church fathers who commented on the two different genealogies of the Lord all agreed that both belonged to Joseph. Since Old Testament genealogies were reckoned from the father's line, the opinion that the genealogy found in Luke is that of Mary was unknown to the early fathers. Julius Africanus, a third-century writer, thought that the Matthew account represented Joseph's actual genealogy. He proposed that Luke registered Joseph's lineage through Heli, his mother's first husband. Heli died childless, however, so Jacob, a relative, married Joseph's mother and "raised up a name" to Heli (Deut. 25:5-10). Therefore, Jesus was officially "supposed" (Luke 3:23) as the son of Joseph, the son of Heli, although Joseph's actual father was Jacob. Julius Africanus's explanation in *Letter to Aristides* was later discussed or endorsed by other early fathers. See Eusebius, *History of the Church,* 1,7; Jerome, *Commentary on Matthew;* and Augustine, *Retract.,* 2,7.

4. For information on Jewish courtship and marriage customs during this period of antiquity, see Fred H. Wright's work, *Manners and Customs of Bible Lands* (Chicago: Moody Press, 1979), 124-34.

5. *The Gospel of the Nativity of Mary,* 1.

6. The phrase "in the sixth month" apparently should be interpreted as "in the sixth month of Elizabeth's pregnancy." This is obvious from Luke 1:24-25 and 1:36; however, some interpret this to be June (sixth month in our Roman calendar) or March (roughly the sixth month after the civil Jewish New Year—Rosh Hashanah) or September (roughly the sixth month in the religious Jewish calendar). Again, such speculation tends not to be productive in determining the birth month of Christ. Based on the traditional date of the nativity (December 25), Roman Catholic, Eastern Orthodox, and many Protestants celebrate March 25 as the date of the annunciation to Mary, but any reliable and conclusive evidence to confirm these traditional dates has yet to surface.

CHAPTER 2

1. For a summary of the life of Augustus in ancient literature consult Suetonius, *The Twelve Caesars: Augustus;* Tacitus, *The Annals;* Nicolaus of Damascus, *The Life of Augustus;* and Augustus summarizing his public career in his *Res Gestae.*

2. Besides the New Testament, the careers of the Herodian rulers of Palestine are largely contained in the works of Flavius Josephus, *The Antiquities of the Jews* and *The Jewish Wars.* A full biography of Herod the Great by his court historian Nicolaus of

Damascus failed to survive the ancient era and is largely lost to us. Fragments of this work, however, have been cited in part in the works of Josephus.

3. Augustus, *Res Gestae*, 13, 25, 34.

4. Josephus, *The Jewish Wars*, 1, 22, 1.

5. Josephus, *Antiquities* and *Jewish Wars* both describe in some detail the Herodian intrafamily intrigues and violence.

6. Macrobius, *Saturnalia*, 2, 4, 11.

7. Josephus, *Antiquities*, 16, 9, 3-4 and 16, 10, 9.

8. Tacitus, *Annals*, 6, 41.

9. Augustus, *Res Gestae*, 8.

10. Tacitus provided this summary in *Annals*, 3, 48. While never mentioning Quirinius as a special "commander for the East," Tacitus did give that title to the man Quirinius tutored—Gaius Caesar—and later to Germanicus under Tiberius. Such an appointment existed all the way back to Mark Anthony. Quirinius probably held this appointment after his consulship with Augustus in 12 B.C. until he tutored Gaius Caesar to take over this role around 2 B.C. Therefore, he could have functioned as a *hegemon* of Syria. *Annals*, 2, 42-43 and 3, 48.

11. Inscription cited by Sir William M. Ramsay, *The Bearing of Recent Discovery on the Trustworthiness of the New Testament* (1915), 285.

12. These inscriptions, discussed by Sir William M. Ramsay in his work, *Was Christ Born in Bethlehem?* (1898; reprinted 1979), 273-74, remain inconclusive in firmly establishing Quirinius as actually governing Syria at the time of the birth of Christ. While even the inscription not naming him seemingly indicates it may be Quirinius, the eroded inscription remains forever incomplete on this detail. It does, however, firmly reveal that this unnamed man governed Syria and Phoenicia twice.

13. This decree was published in a book by Adolf Deissmann, *Light from the Ancient East*, translated by Lionel R. M. Strachen, 4th ed. (New York: 1927), 270-71.

14. Suetonius, *The Twelve Caesars: Augustus*, 94.

CHAPTER 3

1. Luke only mentions one inn (2:7), but Bethlehem probably possessed at least a few places that provided rooms for travelers and guests.

2. Justin Martyr, *Dialogue with Trypho,* 78.

3. Origen, *Against Celsus,* 1, 52.

4. Possibly, Luke could have interviewed Mary and tradition exists that he did; however, the birth accounts ended up rather short and tended to be silent as to many events of the birth and when it actually occurred.

5. Shekalim, 7, 4.

6. Herod the Great ruled Palestine from 40-4 B.C. Josephus mentioned an eclipse of the moon shortly before Herod's death. This eclipse took place on the night of March 12/13, 4 B.C. Herod's successor, Archelaus, slaughtered three thousand people during Passover about a month later. Since the Paschal festivities revolved around the feast on April 11, 4 B.C., we can place the death of Herod sometime between those two confirmed dates. Jesus was born sometime before Herod died. Josephus, *Antiquities,* 17, 6, 4 and *Jewish Wars,* 2, 1, 1-3.

7. Some favor counting Tiberius's coregency with Augustus in A.D. 11/12 as the beginning of his reign and assigning his fifteenth year in A.D. 25/26. The counting of a coregency, however, was not recognized by Roman historians as part of an emperor's reign. Luke, a Gentile who wrote for the citizens and inhabitants of the Roman Empire, followed the custom of reckoning time by the reigns of the emperors like the Roman historians Tacitus and Suetonius. They counted the beginning of Tiberius's reign in A.D. 14, so A.D. 28/29 being the genesis of John's independent ministry is a fairly reliable date. Tacitus, *Annals,* 4, 1. Also see Suetonius, *Twelve Caesars: Life of Tiberius,* 73.

8. Early church speculation on the date of the Nativity of Jesus—Hippolytus, *Commentary on Daniel,* 4, 23, 3; Clement of Alexandria, *Stromata,* 1, 21, 145; and Epiphanius, *Panarion.*

9. For discussion of present practice of sheep herding during the winter months on Palestine, see Paul Maier, *First Christmas* (New York: 1971), 41-42.

10. Mishnah passages: Skekalim, 7, 4 and Bezah, 40a.

11. Justin Martyr, *First Apology,* 34.

CHAPTER 4

1. Joshua or Yeshua can actually mean "Savior," "God's salvation," or "God is salvation." All these variations accurately describe the mission of the Son of God, and the name is most fitting.

2. Even in the days of Jesus, the descendants of the Hebrew tribes were called "Jews" even though some tribal identities remained. Paul was of Benjamin, Barnabas and Zacharias were Levites, and Anna belonged to Asher. After the destruction of the temple in A.D. 70 by the Romans and the further dispersion of the Jewish nation, however, tribal identities became even harder to maintain. Today, all descendants of the Hebrew tribes with the exception of the half-Israelite Palestinian Samaritans are collectively referred to as "Jews."

3. Since the account of Anna specifically mentions her "great age," she could have been more than 84. If an age of 84 represented her years of widowhood, she may have been at least 105 (7 years of marriage plus at least 14 at the time of her marriage). Some commentators even have suggested figures around or over 120. On the other hand, however, 84 was a "great age" in the days that Jesus inhabited this world. Either interpretation is within the realm of possibility.

4. The Luke account in chapter 2 may give the impression that the holy family then returned to Nazareth after the temple visit (v. 39); however, harmony of the Gospels dictate that that reference instead indicates the return from Egypt to Nazareth. Luke chose to leave out the events of the visit of the Magi and the trip to Egypt. When this is understood, there is no conflict between the two birth and early infancy narratives.

CHAPTER 5

1. "We Three Kings of Orient Are" was written and composed by John Henry Hopkins. Hopkins missed the mark in providing his audience with an accurate picture of the Magi and instead simply summarized in song the legends surrounding them. In spite of this, however, the song remains one of the most popular and beloved Christmas carols.

2. Herodotus, *Histories,* 1, 140.

3. Justin Martyr, *Dialogue with Trypho,* 78.

4. Ibid.

5. Suetonius, *Twelve Caesars: Life of Julius Caesar,* 88; and *Life of Nero,* 36.

6. Johannes Kepler, *De Stella Nova* (Prague: 1606).

7. For a more thorough treatment of the planetary conjunction

theory, and for those who have advocated it in part or in whole, see Edersheim, *Life and Times of Jesus the Messiah* (New York: 1923); 1:212-13 (footnotes reveal the theory's major advocates), and Werner Keller, *The Bible As History* (New York: 1956), 345-54.

8. Justin Martyr, *Dialogue with Trypho,* 78.

9. Herodotus, *Histories,* 3, 108.

10. Nothing reliable survives concerning the fate of the Magi after their visit to the Christ child. Much later tradition records that the apostles eventually found them, baptized them, and launched them into missionary careers, but this probably constitutes ecclesiastical storytelling at its worst. Today their holy relics supposedly rest at the Cologne Cathedral, but few regard them as genuine.

CHAPTER 6

1. For a discussion of the last days of Herod the Great, continue to refer to Josephus, *Antiquities* and *Jewish Wars*.

2. Death of the rabbis also derive from Josephus, *Antiquities* and *Jewish Wars*.

3. This story present today in many forms ultimately developed from an account found in the *Arabic Gospel of the Infancy of the Savior,* 23. This recorded legend, however, has little serious historical validity, and the work itself originated from an unknown era long past the second century.

4. Macrobius, *Saturnalia,* 2, 4, 11. Only a few writers have ever dealt with the Herod passage in the *Saturnalia*. It is included in this work with the hope that it can provoke a discussion among both Christian and non-Christian scholars on the validity of the passage in regard to confirming Matthew's account of the slaughter of the innocents.

5. Many Christians observe December 28 as the Feast of the Holy Innocents, however, like many Christian holidays, no date can actually be pinpointed as the very day of Herod's murder of the children of Bethlehem. For Paul Maier's estimate of the number of slaughtered infants, see his fine work, *First Christmas* (New York: 1971), 84.

6. Josephus, *Jewish Wars,* 1, 30-33.

7. The material concerning the reign of Archelaus again comes from Josephus, *Antiquities* and *Jewish Wars*.

CHAPTER 7

1. Josephus, *Jewish Wars*, 1, 4 and 5 for the anarchy in Galilee and the revolt of Judas Ben-Hezekiah and the destruction of Sepphoris. This Judas may also be the Judas of Galilee who later revolted once again in A.D. 7 at the time of Quirinius's provincial census and taxing.

2. For Herod Antipas the Tetrarch's early reign and Judas the Galilean's revolt in Galilee at the time of Quirinius' census in A.D. 7, see Josephus, *Antiquities*, 18, 1 and 2.

3. Josephus, *Against Apion*, 2, 26.

4. As evidenced by Mark 14:70, Galileans like Simon Peter were distinguished by their dialect. Apparently, Judeans looked at the Galileans in contempt for, among other things, their corrupted dialect.

5. Events of the end of the reign of Archelaus and the census and taxing of Quirinius derive from Josephus, *Antiquities*, 17, 13 and 18, 1.

CHAPTER 8

1. For Tiberius and his policy toward the Jews see Josephus, *Antiquities*, 18, 3, 1-5; Tacitus, *Annals*, 2, 85; and Suetonius, *Twelve Caesars: Tiberius*, 36.

2. Josephus, *Antiquities*, 18, 2, 2 for a succession of Roman governors and high priests in Judea during the reign of Tiberius.

3. For Josephus on Herod Philip II see *Antiquities*, 18, 2, 1 and also *Antiquities*, 18, 4, 6.

4. Ibid., 18, 2, 3.

5. For information on the Lord's family after the ascension of Jesus, we are largely dependent on the writings of the early church fathers. Eusebius, the early church historian, recorded that many close family members in addition to those cited in Ch. 8 survived into the second century. Among them, he revealed that sons of Jude, the half-brother of Jesus, lived well into the reign of the Roman emperor Trajan (A.D. 98-117). Eusebius, *The History of the Church*, 2-3.

Third-century writer Julius Africanus wrote that the extended family of the Lord remained in Nazareth and other nearby locales for some time after His ascension. Apparently honored by the early church, "the Master's family" could have provided a wealth of information to the Gospel writers, however, while the Evangelists may have interviewed them concerning the Lord's life, we are never informed that they did. Julius Africanus, *Letter to Aristides* should be consulted for information on both the Lord's family, as well as the ancestors of the Lord.

6. Justin Martyr, *Dialogue with Trypho*, 88.

7. The Greek Septuagint version of the Old Testament was rather widespread in the Greek East. Fragments and partial books of these Greek Scriptures have been found in Palestine, and this perhaps suggests that Palestinian Jews made wider use of the Septuagint than once thought.

8. Eusebius, *History of the Church,* 7, 18.

9. See note 7 of Ch. 3 for an explanation of this chronology.

10. The day of Jesus' baptism by John remains unknown, however, it is traditionally celebrated on or shortly after the Epiphany feast day of January 6. His journey to the Jordan probably began only a day or two before His actual baptism day.

CONCLUSION

1. Tactius, *Annals,* 3, 22-23, 48.

2. Josephus, *Antiquities,* 18, 7, 1-2.

3. See Tacitus, *Annals,* and Seutonius, *Life of Tiberius,* for a more complete summary of the life of Tiberius.